MEMO'S FOR LEADERS

I0391060

Nikola M. Susnjar

For Mom & Dad

CONTENTS

INTRODUCTION

This is not a text book. Leading is not a science. Leadership never will be part of a larger scientific category. This art of handling people is broader and more subjective than any other discipline that exists. This is why we cannot put our finger on defining it.

The essential error in trying to define leaders is that we assume they are all the same. However much we lump these individuals together we see that their qualities and experiences differ from each other as we differ from them. This is why there are unlimited examples of leadership in history that expresses greatness and failure in the same amounts.

The fight to duplicate great leaders has been a task for many these last few decades. To emulate the DNA of greatness and effectiveness is impossible if looked at as scientific approach. The reality of training programs and seminars that many corporations use is that many of these 'leadership trainees' do not want this responsibility to begin with. Others lack courage and willpower to continue leading.

Many lack the integrity to lay down their reputations to lead effectively. This and many other factors influence the inability to replicate leadership substance.

This is why we must look at the other end of the leadership spectrum. Not as a scientific subject, but as a realistic changing entity. The displays of leading can be seen in the animal as well as the human. Only the parts of the natural genetic process or 'higher power' can a leader be called to a role. Either out of necessity for survival or for the pleasure of serving. In this, it starts changing itself for the environment regardless of feast or famine.

For example, a leader will choose to take the reins of the group if they see that the survival of the group is being threatened. They communicate the message to the group, they first take the steps to move the group forward, afterwards they monitor the safety and ultimately bring them to it. It is part of human nature to survive, nowadays, we just have the ability to take action sooner than before with educating ourselves better about what good leadership does.

This small escort about the various leaders in history was meant to be as short as possible. It was supposed to outline just the basic information necessary to understand who the 99 leaders in history were and what they wanted to say-imprint to the world. Their actions are written down here briefly. Some messages might seem repeated, however, the leaders that have these messages were different in their time.

None of what you read in these short few pages will be new. Hopefully what you read will be a reminder, just organized in a different way.

The way we see and think about leading needs to be reassessed. There are actually little if any experts on leading. Why? Like we mentioned before, it is not a static discipline that is rigid, where it stays the same. The principles that keep getting redefined, keep changing over time. Their foundations might keep a wobbly constant but it never stays the same in a single generation that it can be duplicated, only synthesized into interpretations.

This is why we must *think* about leading, not just learn it like a classical textbook course. Examples of poor leadership and the results it creates are all around us. We need only look at local schooling or even parenting to see poor leadership examples. Actively participating in assessment of our own actions is the first step to anything. This is what this book is about. You must first center yourself in order to continue with others. All of the examples in this book, are of characters who first took themselves into account before others. A selfish but necessary action in order to effectively lead. Thinking is a self centered act that is a requirement in leading.

This book can be read straight through or in chunks or flipped to certain pages. It was not meant to have any chronological order, nor is any leader more significant than the other. Every individual here has displayed some kind of value that has brought prosperity in one form or another.

Out of everything that is written here, none of it will be useful if the messages are not put in practice. The action is what is important to leading. Since the non-static nature of leading means that the knowledge we use and the examples we see; we understand them first, but then it is up to us to use this information.

1. CONFUCIUS (KONGFUZI) (551-479) BCE

Famous quote:
"Our greatest glory is not in never falling, but in rising every time we fall."

'Master Kong' or Confucius or better yet the movement Confucianism, has been around for more than 2000 years and is still practiced today. While many of the works are debatable because of literary sources, it is undeniable that Confucius made his messages and beliefs known through the work that he did. In doing -Walk the talk.

The message:

Be compassionate in dealings with others.

Confucius made it very relevant, that his teachings, are focused on the union of the whole group. That the individual has to make it upon themselves to work within the society and people that they exist in. Leadership therefore is in the same context. The leader(s) must adapt to the people and serve them as a person who promotes harmony and peace rather than oppression and authority. That the duties of the leader are part of the world in which they live.

Interpretations for success:

Compassion in leading doesn't have to be a soft, and fuzzy process. It means that you open your mind to ideas that others bring to you. You do not see threats, you see opportunities to work with others. You do not condemn you help, and solve. You take the first step in initiating a hard talk to others about where you are.

To change in the 21st century, Leadership needs to continue to practice the Confucian way of life. Leading with the whole group in mind is the peak of teamwork and cooperation. Picture the leader as a person who is pulling the group not the one in the back pushing.

2. JESUS OF NAZARETH (4 BCE-30 AD)

Famous quote:
"But seek ye first the kingdom of God, and his righteousness; and all these things shall be added unto you." Matthew 6:33

If there are a top 3 list of leaders in history that have influenced the personality of the world, then Jesus would be on this list. Regardless of the information we have, it is undeniable that a man who through his work in Imperial Rome made a movement of peace in a time of war.

The message:

Hope for the future.

The summary of the whole literary works of the bible, are stories that teach and inspire hope for many. When the collection of the new and old testament is combined there is an underlying message, that in times of oppression there will always be optimism at the end of tunnel. The works of Jesus and his purpose on his journey was to provide hope. It is fitting that his mission was all the more important considering the oppression that the Roman Empire held over their absolute territory.

Interpretations for success:

A leader if anything, must be the one who is positive of the future. If they are to lead anyone, they need to possess the positive expectations that the results will eventually come, (when the hard work and creativity and other things are taken into consideration) regardless of time frame. Hope is hard to define, that is why many people give up. Hope is also related to experience, a leader who has experienced similar situations before will have more hope, which is related to positive expectancy of the future.

The lesson from Jesus here is that even if the whole group is "hopeless", it is a rule that the leader is not. You try new things, you investigate, you move from your current post and think. You do what is necessary to find out where you are going. This process is the process of hope, never stopping to believe that you can accomplish what you started.

3. DOGEN ZENJI (1200-1253)

Famous quote:
"Prefer to be defeated in the presence of the wise man, than to excel among fools."

The Shobogenzo was Dogen's most famous work. A collection of 95 essays. A philosopher of Buddhism and practitioner of enlightenment. His main points sought to teach others that peace is the way of life. Having peace with one self and the actions that one does. That it is not things, or others that bring peace and progress but the self-initiated mind.

The message:

Accept the world as it is.

Not just Dogen, but many religions and philosophers emphasize the point of realization of the self and the environment around. We cannot control the natural surroundings of the planet, not even the actions of government, not even the people we work with, even our family. We can only control what is us. This oversimplified notion of enlightenment is very difficult to achieve especially in our modern-competitive and consumerist world. To not want, and not desire is foreign and uncomfortable.

Interpretations for success:

The way for a leader then, is to recognise that they can only try, and work on themselves as being a model for others. If the right actions lead to results then great, if they don't then great too. A practicing leader always learns from victories and even more so from defeats. There are no shortcuts in the trailblazer's world, they work to seek understanding not profits (profits are just by-products of successful leading).

As Dogen wrote, "first work on your inward being in order to influence the outward environment".

4. GHANDI (1869-1950)

Famous quote:
"The weak can never forgive. Forgiveness is the attribute of the strong."

Through a deep sense of pride and self-reflection, Ghandi realized that much of his life will be fought for others and not himself. First hand witnessing the racism and prejudice that was happening around him in the late 1800's he saw the need for reforms. He believed that education of the children was of upmost importance in building a better society in India.

The message:

Don't hold a grudge.

As the life of Ghandi progressed, there were more and more examples of inequality among the classes both in material and spiritual forms. Where hatred and violence were commonplace. It was in this environment that Ghandi saw the need to make an adjustment, even if that meant that he would do it himself, regardless of the imposed and likely adversities that will occur because of this attitude. His results are documented in history as one of the most influential peace movements of all time.

Interpretations for success:

If one humble man, who valued life of others more than his own, can let go of hatred towards him, it would seem a small price to pay for our own much smaller situations. We should not be so vain in life to think that someone who has done us wrong, or a situation that has happened not in our favor is a direct attack on us. We are more often than not; collateral damage of the environmental/behavioral circumstances we find ourselves in.

If someone does you wrong, think of them as being out of their element. Even if they do hold a grudge against you, it is in your interest not to waste any more energy or time on them. You figured them out, great! Move on and live your life. Find a way around them or avoid them all together. Whatever the case, spend time on solving problems not on political games or office foreplay.

5. THE BUDDHA (563-483) BCE

Famous quote:
"Give, even if you only have a little."

Sidhartha Gautama, more commonly known as the Buddha, was a practical thinker who emphasized the salvation of the human spirit and the behaviour of daily life. Having been born in a well to do family and lifestyle, Buddha really had no reason to leave the life of comfort. It was through a vision, however, that he decided to leave everything behind and discover the source of earthly "pain" and suffering. Living frugally and with little, he reached enlightenment several years after. The philosophy of 'action without action' and *thought* which precedes individual existence, made Buddha enlightened.

The message:

Whatever you think you know, share it.

The world would be a different place if many of the people such as Buddha kept the information they had about life, business, people, existence a secret. That simply existing is not enough, and that which we know is not all we know about that subject as a whole. Enlightenment is not a destination but a way of life and a journey until death. Meant to be shared with others.

Interpretations for success:

As a leader, you will be faced with situations that seem banal and easy. Simply speaking about them may seem foolish and stupid, at least in your mind. The truth is different. Many of the situations are unique across multidisciplinary and globalized realms. Things that worked in one industry we might say, might not work in another. Which is not true.

Whatever you know, no matter how small it is, should be used for the construction of new ideas and creative solutions. This is not just for the group you are with, it is more for yourself, your own enlightenment in that subject which is not yet fully discovered. Only by giving something to the world can you take something back.

6. ST. FRANCIS OF ASSISI (1181-1226)

Famous quote:
"The deeds you do may be the only sermon some persons will hear today."

An entrepreneur in his own right, St. Francis began his journey of finding God by himself. Born into a well off family, he decided to live the life similar to Jesus Christ and live in poverty. He later got accepted by the Catholic Church as they saw his cause just and virtuous. His message was simple to his followers, to live and follow the teachings of Jesus Christ.

The message:

Walk the talk.

Few people in history have had the self-initiated drive to become something great, furthermore something great which does not involve money. Whether it was God speaking to him or his own desire to change the world he was living in, St. Francis believed that all things, living and dead had a connection to one another and treated them the same. His mission was to exemplify the Christ way of living, not through scripture alone but in the way a person lived, frugally and without desires to worldly possessions. His success in this made him a icon of the time.

Interpretations for success:

Leadership at the most basic level is a test towards the individual using it. The people who are to follow the leader are actually testing them… always. Seeing if they walk the talk. Leaders who preach change and unity around the organization, but fail to do it themselves raise contempt and chaos than the leaders who are the fore runners for these requirements.

Like St. Francis, you say that you will do something, but more importantly you act out and become the change you preach. There is a dimension of solidarity and peace when a leader shows the actions that they want done in their followers, how can you not follow someone who is actually doing it. Learn from the master St. Francis, that any deed must be followed by action and not conversation.

7. SUNZI (SUN TZU) (544-496) BCE

Famous quote:
"Know thy self, know thy enemy. A thousand battles, a thousand victories."

Even the conflicting ideas of historical origin and timeline of Sun Tzu cannot deny that the advice on strategy and planning are timeless. His approach to life, through a practical guide to warfare for the Emperor of China makes him a celebrity even today. Many Chinese leaders both ancient and modern has accredited at least a portion of their influence and decision making on his book "The Art of War". It is not the book that is most interesting but the figure in history that made it possible to change an realm through knowing yourself and knowing your enemy as the recipe for success.

The message:

Know what you want.

Sun Tzu emphasized the importance of knowing what you want out of yourself. Is it quick victory, is it total annihilation or is it embarrassment of the other army? Better yet, avoiding conflict is more important than engaging in it. He emphasizes that knowing how to avoid conflict all together and subdue an enemy without drawing your sword is a greater victory in itself. Only the wisest of military leaders promote avoiding battle(s) and engaging in peace.

Interpretations for success:

While your battle will not be fought with the sword or gun, you will have to make a decision to confront people who wish to overturn your work. If you do not know where you are going or what you want out of your, team, company, children, others will make the decisions for you. This is in itself a form or warfare, the imposed will of others on you and your life. Be careful not to let them do this.

To make significant change in your life and your business, you the leader, must perform like Sun Tzu. Not engaging in conflict but diffusing it wherever possible. If the inevitable does happen and you are forced to collide with someone you will be ready because you spent the hours and years preparing for the fight around the corner. The thousands of battles that you will encounter will mean nothing since you have made the decision to know who you are and what is important to you.

8. J.P. MORGAN (1837-1913)

It is a rare occurrence that one person can save a nation from crisis. J.P. (John Pierpont) Morgan did just that amongst the Panic of 1907, in which he infused a substantial amount of his own capital to save America from economic collapse. Through the consolidation and acquisition of numerous industrial and other business ventures, Pierpont made a more cost effective, faster distribution, and higher output production industry for America.

The message:

Your resolve as a leader must be the strongest in the group.

Riddled with controversy over monopolizing early 1900's America, J.P. Morgan and Co made significant changes in the output of American society. The investments that were made on behalf of advancement, were only able by magnate's such as Pierpont. The media that was associated with his fame was also connected to his failures. Regardless, the resolve that J.P. Morgan had made America a very different place if he hadn't been there.

Interpretations for success:

The goal should never be, to raise something so spectacular as to change the world, it should be to endure, until…

A leaders resolve, especially through numerous failures and debacles, personal and professional, needs to be clad in iron. Unbreakable. Unrelenting until the goal is achieved. We would have a very different picture of leadership if people gave up on the first sign of trouble, which is a very natural thing to do. Be the 1% of people who endure and have a resolve so huge that even the 'American' economy cannot stop them.

9. HENRY FORD (1863-1947)

Cinderella's story, might not have any weight when we talk about Henry Ford. From humble beginnings on a farm to the climb of the corporate ladder with the Edison Illuminating Company, Ford never gave up. The billionaire Ford and his audacity to try and create a gasoline powered engine could only have come from divine inspiration and years of hard work. Trial and error should be associated with an innovator such as Ford, whose company survived a century of bad economy, war, depression, recession, stock market collapse, massive competition. Not only is such a story rare, but inspirational to anyone who practices leadership.

The message:

You, can be the only person who decides that you failed, no one else.

Being imposed by others to do their way of working made Ford irritable, often misjudged.

It was in his tenacity that the Model T came about, with a lot of meddling from others the car was a success unprecedented to date. With the majority of Americans learning to drive on it back in the day.

Interpretations for success:

For a leader, there needs to be a higher calling other than just, monetary gains. Ford is an example of someone who wanted something more than money. He wanted to change the world. He did it with transportation. A gasoline engine. What then is a leader if not a trailblazer and change maker? Many can imitate an image of humbleness, toughness, tenacity and the like, but eventually they are seen through their superficial costume.

It is not a simple task to just seek knowledge, wisdom and change, often in the forms of failing. Failure will most likely meet you at every step. Failure will entice your comfort zone. Failure will call you to rest and take it easy. What is it in this time, when you start doubting yourself that you will say to yourself? It only takes a second to give in...

...it only takes a second to push forward.

10.MATSUSHITA KONOSUKE (1894-1989)

Famous quote:
"You may be a well-educated clever and virtuous person, but those qualities will not necessarily make you a successful businessman. You must give your best to each and every task you take on, and reflect on your performance with an honest and unprejudiced eye."

For many Japanese, Konosuke, the founder of Panasonic was considered "the god of management". His life story, a hard climb uphill from poverty and hunger to becoming an electrical inspector with the Osaka Electrical Light Company to becoming the founder of one of the biggest electronics companies in history is a testament to his resilience for living.

The message:

Maximum effort…. always.

In racing, running or motorsports, they say that the start is most important to get right, exerting the maximum to get a lead. Konosuke would argue that it is the consistency in your actions that you should look at, throughout your life and career. Starting is easy, you can stop whenever you want if things are looking bad. Going until you get it right is hard. For this you need maximum attention to your actions.

Interpretations for success:

It is not enough to just start. Leadership is not a "touch" football sport, where you stop when you score. Maximum exertion is required in your most banal tasks. Understanding why they exist in your repertoire, who are they useful for, who can use them on your team. All of this cognitive activity directed towards a more effective leadership and management process.

You will not be successful as leader if you dabble in it. As Konosuke, you must relish the opportunity to learn and be better in your field. You must create an atmosphere where others feel the same need to exert their maximum towards their work. To do this, do as Konosuke did, he never stopped doing because he loved his work. This secret you should share with your followers.

11.PETER DRUCKER (1909-2005)

Famous quote:
"Effective leadership is not about making speeches or being liked; leadership is defined by results not attributes."

The father of modern management and the modern business model, Peter Drucker shaped the way companies look at their business. Thought of more as a guru of management than anything else, his experience was formed through the toughest times in modern history, economic and global. His work in economics and management shaped the concepts of how to govern a corporation.

The message:

You will be judged by your results first, then your personality.

In the real world, people often will look at the face value of things/people/events. Judge you by your appearance, give you ten seconds to make a first impression. Sad but true. It is rare nowadays that someone gives more thought to the results part of their work more than the elbow rubbing with their superiors. Drucker emphasized the importance of quality management and leadership in all parts of the corporation, results in the end are what make or break a company not smiles and pat's on the back.

Interpretations for success:

If you know you put more emphasis on appearance in your company than you do in actual performance, you need to re-evaluate. Leave the company because they are doomed, or re align yourself to true management values.

Do not neglect courtesy and manners for the sake of results, however, the focus needs to be on bringing value in one form or another. Optimizing or creating in the company or just plain doing a good job can be said to someone who cares about results. Not fiddling idly around the office, not wandering aimlessly all day, not conversing on the phone 'pretending' its work related. Hate un-productivity and messy work; set an example for others in that they see the old art of being at work and working rather than withering away in life 8 hrs a day.

12. JACK WELCH (1935-)

Famous quote:
"Good business leaders create a vision, articulate the vision, passionately own the vision, and relentlessly drive it to completion."

It is hard to believe that a monstrously successful executive like Welch, could have any criticism. As the popular internet slogan goes, "Haters gonna hate", for Welch who in his ten years as head of GE grew the company 4000% it is going to create some "haters". We can all learn a thing or two from the leadership giant who was named "Manager of the Century" by fortune magazine.

The message:

Vision. Know where you are heading.

It is difficult to see the forest from the trees, guru's and sages might say to us. It is then, all the more important to know where you are and what you want. The most successful leaders might not know exactly the outcome of their future experiences but they see that outline that helps them define the actual place when it arrives. To have vision like Welch you must know your stuff and be confident enough to take on superman when he shows up to stop you. This is the only way you can be sure that you are heading in the right direction.

Interpretations for success:

Faith is a product of having vision. Strategy is something totally different than vision and faith. Vision transcends ourselves and moves into the future where strategy has not yet arrived. All of us want 'something', but is it strong enough for us to keep thinking about it day in day out. It is too easy to want something; it must have an emotional connection with us.

True leadership vision needs to have some pain associated with it. Companies might have poor bottom lines, and modest performing KPI's etc. For people it might be unbalanced lifestyles and relationships, for aspiring leaders it might be lack of experience. If the vision cannot associate itself with a present, painful emotion then *It* will not last. We must be connected to the vision on another level in order for us to keep it with us, and no matter what comes up we will always remember why we set out to grab and complete this vision

13. HENRY MINTZBERG (1939-)

Famous quote:
"Learning is not doing; it is reflecting on doing."

For Canadian, Professor Henry Mintzberg Ph.D, management is a activity of doing not just reading and crunching numbers. Too much emphasis on the technical parts of managing and strategizing will dull the senses to the true nature of management; to handle. With a globalized economy of increasing complexity, it is not the manager who is smart but the one who is adaptable that will be successful. Professor Mintzberg has been a pioneer in the management and leadership debate for over 50 years.

The message:
Your strategy doesn't start until you get off your ass.

If we could lump all people into two categories it would be 90% strategists and the other 10% who actually get things done. It is too easy to be a strategist nowadays. Just draw two dots and connect them and you know just about as much as anybody else in strategy. Doing the actions that are necessary is a whole different story.

Interpretations for success:

Once you figure out what it is that your company must do to undertake changes, and decision making, you need to start actually executing the program asap. Often too, individual tasks are part of this never ending strategy. When it comes from the top to the actual employee that should do the work, the strategy stops.

Why?

You have set unclear direction, its too complicated. Too much detail and jargon. You're pretending to be smart to the employee etc. We then wait for the strategy to happen. It never does the way we thought it would. The main reason being is that we are *not* ourselves involved in the process of it, we have hidden motives and ego driven positions that break the cycle of executing the plan. It's simple, strategy is like listening. One pound of listening to an ounce of talking. *One pound of working for an ounce of strategy.*

14. MICHAEL PORTER (1947-)

Famous quote:
"The essence of strategy is choosing what not to do."

Today it is hard to not know who Michael Porter is and what he stands for. Especially in the world of commerce and business. Known for strategy and his way of integrating the intellectual to the practical he has become one of the most cited authors in business and economics.

The message:

Know what you do NOT want.

Experience, it is said is the best teacher. Strategy then is the precursor to having less pain in experience. Even if you fail at something, if you have had some strategy and planned a bit in advance the idea might still be salvageable. Knowing what and where and how much is a part of strategic behavior that involves not just you but the competitors in your branch of business.

Interpretations for success:

Part of being a impressive leader is to know when to say no. Better yet it is knowing when to quit while you're ahead. Or stopping when you have reached you goal and not over doing it. This is something that 'winner's' cannot understand. They keep going until they fall flat on their faces, or lose more than they have gained by over extending.

All too often we get placed in positions that we really do not feel like doing. Picking up the pieces of others is most often the case, however, this is a good test for your leadership. It is also a bad test to not knowing where you are in life. You sometimes need to stand up for yourself and say no, rather, say no with a reason behind it, and "that's not my job" doesn't count. It needs to be a real reason.

15.BILL GATES (1955-)

Famous quote:
"Success is a lousy teacher. It seduces smart people
into thinking they can't lose."

The shape of our society and its behavior is largely due to businesses that made the necessary changes such as Microsoft. Bill Gates is often seen as the richest man on earth, give or take a spot or two. It is not his money that made him famous, but his innovative way of bringing solutions to the world that gave him the power to move markets.

The message:

Never get high on your own success/fame etc.

Even super geniuses learn to keep going. Bill Gates is one such person. Regardless of the success he has had, and what we have obviously seen, it is the unseen that is more important. That people like Gates have a clean sheet of un failed efforts is untrue. You yourself need to double your success rate by doubling your failure rate.

Interpretations for success:

It is in living on the high of being in the center of attention that many lose sight of the true original goal. You might have a hot streak one year and a total flop the next. If you are not prepared, then be ready for lots of pain that follows hot headedness.

Learn to be humble and quiet your ego, fast. It is a hard thing to control especially if you are talented in a skill or job. To hide your talent from others is hard and uncomfortable, however, others will resent you for your skills even undermine your efforts behind your back. It is better than to work on the skill to master it beyond your capabilities; make yourself even better. Never inflate beyond recommended guidelines.

16.PLATO (427-347) BCE

Famous quote:
"Wise men speak because they have something to say; fools because they have to say something."

His work reaches millennia as well as through dogma, where his philosophy influenced Saints as well as emperors. Plato worked for Socrates his teacher then he taught Aristotle who in turn taught Alexander the Great. Having a golden touch so powerful as to influence geographical territories through war and conquest is the closest a mortal can wish for to becoming divine.

The message:

Speak only when you have something to say.

Even today Plato is considered a mega mind of philosophy. Having to spare words then is counterproductive, even for Plato. To have that much influence in a branch of knowledge a person needs to be still and be able to think critically and creatively. Speaking only hinders this process, bludgeoning the mind.

Interpretations for success:

If you are asked something, answer. If you know something, tell it. There is little room for interpretation when leading people. It is far more productive to listen than to do speeches. Listening is a form of speaking, but in your cognitive space.

Ask yourself, what would I gain by talking about this? If the answer is, "not much", don't bother. Keep it to yourself you'll look smarter.

17. ARISTOTLE (384-322) BCE

Famous quote:
"Quality is not an act, it is a habit."

Teaching must be one of the hardest jobs in the world. It is even harder when you have ambitious students who won't back down. Aristotle had this problem when facing a young boy named Alexander. This boy would later conquer the known world. Aristotle then must have had some essential quality in his work with Alexander, for he produced a war machine capable of genius.

The message:

Emphasize building quality.

For Aristotle it was not enough to just show up to work, he came to make a difference. The life he lead was one of utmost diligence to future generations and he knew it. That his work would influence the minds of the world he would not see. His work was built on the strongest of foundations that are used even today by you and me.

Interpretations for success:

Ever heard the saying, "if you're gonna do something, do it right.", probably. Quality is a scarce commodity in a hyper consumerist society such as ours. We are dazzled by products that are produced with utmost love and care, as well as people who produce by their talents. This is ever true in leadership. If you're going to lead, lead properly and correctly.

Quality in leadership is more than a calculated measurement, it has little to do with mathematics and KPI's. It is more visceral in nature. We can automatically tell as humans when we see someone who cares about us, or who is willing to lay on the line for us. This is a by-product of leadership quality, but it is not the only product. Such as teachers, leaders need to emulate their qualities into their followers and other leaders, not to do so robs the leader and future generations of actually moving ahead.

18.CICERO (106- 43) BCE

Julius Caesar praised Cicero in saying, "it is more important to have greatly extended the frontiers of the Roman spirit, rather than the frontiers of the Roman empire.". It is not by accident that Cicero was and still is being remember for his ability to convey a message properly, something which he worked very hard at to master.

The message:

When presenting, present from experience and knowledge not improvisation.

The way we speak to others is often wrong. We talk about nonsense, and things that just fill empty time between pauses of a conversation. Or a conversation that is supposed to happen. It is rare that we will have something smart to say to someone or somebody to us. It almost seems unreal when we start speaking with someone who has a gem of information or experience they share with us. We become enchanted and engaged.

Interpretations for success:

Always think before you compile your next sentence. It is too easy to have a loose tongue and very often dangerous. Do not just speak for filling silence. If the group is silent then you too should be, unless you have something of value to add. If you do not, be quiet.

Too many quotes and sayings exist that silence is golden. Where when we hear a sage or guru speak they directly get to the point. Using as little words as possible to convey the message. Much like Cicero you should convey your point to your boss and colleagues with substantial eloquence and concrete information.

19.JULIUS CAESAR (100-44) BCE

Famous quote:
"As a rule, men worry more about what they can't see than about what they can."

The Roman Republic ended with him and the Roman Empire started through him. It is debatable and senseless to discuss if he was good or bad for the people. What matters is that he set in motion events that would cut the world up into Roman and everybody else.

The message:

Power stays only with those who are prepared to have it.

When leaders start on the path of moving their followers to a goal, they need to be aware like Julius Caesar of what will happen. Probably a lot of blood will be spilt in the process of creating something or changing something altogether. While no blood is being spilt in corporate environments it is evident that economic carnage exists with Caesar's renamed into "CEO's".

Interpretations for success:

Are you prepared to face the decisions that you make today, tomorrow when they go wrong? Be very certain that bad decisions you make will cost you (and everyone around you) emotional and psychological stress. Power in leadership is not forgiving, it is messy and brutal in nature. Your moves will influence not just your followers but their families.

If you are not yet ready to accept a role in leading, that you know will cost you more than you will gain, pause for a better time. It makes no difference to you losing valuable time in repairing your reputation, because of poor decisions and bad attitudes, than in being ready for the role. Power is synonymous with leading, you are given power by leading, only if you have the capability to handle that power should you lead.

Imagine a 16 year old with a turbo charged sports car and you get the idea…

20. AUGUSTUS OCTAVIUS CAESAR (63 BCE- 14 AD)

Being famously wealthy and in good standing with Julius Caesar, Augustus Octavian Caesar remolded Rome for the better. In a long time, there existed Pax Romana (The Roman Peace) while Augustus was in charge. Revisiting new frontiers and challenges he introduced, roads, the Praetorian guard, official police and fire fighters in the new Rome.

The message:

Patience is a weapon.

With the amount of murder and political turmoil in Rome during the rise of Augustus, the 'would be' Emperor of Rome possessed unrivaled patience. Knowing when to move aside, and learning when to strike at his foes, solidified his position in moving into power. Only with patience was he able to see the whole picture of Roman complexity in front of him and lay siege on his enemies.

Interpretations for success:

Ask yourself, how long would it take to swim across the world? Probably impossible. That is how some people behave, at impossibilities, and no matter what you do with them, they will never change. The best weapon you can have with them is patience, both in giving decisions to them and in receiving their decisions. Don't negate, don't react. Just listen and be slow to decide.

The same is for your own way of life. Is it really going to hurt you not to answer that email at 8 o'clock at night? What does it mean to you now, neglecting other things (such as family, or friends) in order to chase nonsense that can wait?

While everybody else is killing themselves and each other, you have the presence of mind to sit back and wait for their episodes to end. You just walk over the bodies to your goal when they are done. Learn to endure.

21.HANNIBAL BARCA (247-182) BCE

Famous quote:
"We will either find a way or make one."

The term great leader, what does it really mean? If you had to put it into a person's name, as one of the greatest in history, then you should put it into Hannibal's. The only opposition to the most powerful entity at the time, with limited resources and only wit and courage to act, Hannibal placed Rome, many times in a state of emergency. The mere mention of his name was enough to set Roman citizens into hiding.

The message:

Reputation is worth more than all the money in the world.

Fearless, and set on revenge, the amount of vengeance that Hannibal set lose on Roman legions literally made them bathe in blood time and again. It was not his brutality that made him a legend in Rome and Carthage, but it was his guile and courage that solidified the reputation of Hannibal.

Interpretations for success:

You will never make enough money to influence everyone you want to. Reputation on the other hand is free, but not free in the sense that you 'just get it'. Reputation is the 'force' behind the leader. Where you do not even have to introduce yourself and everyone knows what you are about, your name speaks for you even without you saying a thing.

Every move you make in your career marks a spot on your reputation. If you make silly mistakes it takes you backward, if you make lots - you tarnish it, where you must start over. Good reputations are hard to hold, jealousy and arrogance from others will try to destroy your reputation while 'trying' to build theirs. It is in this that you must be more, competence, harder working, smarter, nicer, and compelling to lead than your poisoned competitors.

22.ST AUGUSTINE OF HIPPO (354-430)

Famous quote:
"Do you wish to be great? Then begin by being.
Do you desire to construct a vast and lofty fabric?
Think first about the foundations of humility.
The higher your structure is to be, the deeper
must be its foundation."

Writing, De Civitate Dei contra Paganos or The City of God, St. Augustine helped formulate what is now Christian philosophy and doctrine. The original builders after the fall of the Roman Empire of the Catholic church, his teachings and work represent a new era of living in a post Roman world.

The message:

Live with grace. There exists something greater than yourself.

You should not be so preoccupied with how people think of you. St Augustine made sure that after the fall of the Roman empire the laws regarding children slaves and infanticide were known as terrible challenges that were being ignored. Only when you transcend yourself and your own 'false idol' that you can live for the betterment of your community.

Interpretations for success:

It is too easy to spot phoney leaders. We can figure them out in a heartbeat. They are televised, and experienced in the workplace all too often. It is then a shock when a leader which transcends themselves and their own goals to help others that we are frozen with awe for them. Mother Teresa or Nelson Mandela stories captivate our souls not just our minds, for we cannot image ourselves going through the same to benefit the community. We are too poor spiritually to do this, in other words we lack grace.

Only when you have figured out your mission in "life" can you contemplate how you can live a leadership life of grace; the community before you. It seems like an impossible ask from a time where people in power are grabbing and getting theirs left right and center. Businesses are destroying the environment, and financiers are drowning us in debt. Can you lift yourself above the 'noise' and truly help or will you be like the rest. The grace you seek will set the rest of these bad characteristics in meaningless thought.

23. ASHOKA (304-232) BCE

Famous quote:
"No society can prosper if it aims at making things easier- instead it should aim at making people stronger."

It is rare that power is shared with religion. Ashoka was considered one of India's greatest rulers. He consolidated many aspects of religion, politics, state and the people under his rule. After war, it was peace that ruled with Ashoka.

The message:

Pray that things are not easier, pray that you become stronger.

It is often the case, with rulers and emperors, that after years of blood they find peace. For the famous ruler Ashoka, he turned to Buddhism to balance his conquered lands. That not through force or violence but through peace was his strategic focus to rule. To change yourself into something different is the image of true strength.

Interpretations for success:

Years of fighting and battles, at work and at home, will make you weak. Most of all you will be weak mentally. Drained of all the power you had when you were young and determined to take on the world. Society and the meddling of others will deplete your will to continue fighting. It is in this discovery, that you will find the chains that bind your progress.

When you discover that you have been taken advantage of, it is vital to break free. Either challenging yourself to continue and break through the mess you are in, or continue on a totally different path. Anything but staying in a state of ease or complacency. Half of the strength you need is in starting anew.

24.IMMANUEL KANT (1724-1804)

Kant's point of view is most easily recognized in "can't live with them, can't live without them." Philosophy where he mentions social unsociability for human beings. His work constructed modern philosophy, of which he never intended to do. The mind was Kant's sole focus, maybe his years as a tutor with 1 on 1 experience gave him the insight that others did not have.

The message:

Whatever you say you will do, do it.

The idea's that Kant played with underscore leadership abilities and qualities today. The notion of synthesizing something for the sake of conversation is useless. The example Kant gives is, when a person borrows money and promises to pay it back, but has no intention to do so. This then defeats the purpose of making promises, especially if everyone acted this way. Leaders who promise but never deliver are not leaders.

Interpretations for success:

Assess the commitment you are about to make to your team. If you feel that you won't be able to deliver a request from someone then say so. Don't say you will do it when you think you cannot. If you do, the person will be happy, but if you say you will and don't the reputation you have made will disappear.

The trust that you will build with people, as in Kant's writing, which is defined by the environment and experiences that the mind registers over time. The trust is actually a made up 'thing', it is more fear control than trust. The less people fear that you will take advantage of them the more they will 'trust' your intentions to help them and the groups cause.

25.FRIEDRICH   NIETZSCHE (1844-1900)

Famous quote:
"There is always some madness in love. But there is also always some reason in madness."

While he would later in his life break down mentally, the same brilliance that made his name famous would be the same that would cause him great pain. Nietzsche was a professor at Basel in Switzerland for many years, producing some of psychologies greatest work. It was the study of the conscience that made him construct a new paradigm of the mind.

The message:

Learn to love your job, your team, your enemies, yourself.

Only in constructing our thoughts can we fully understand our reality. A concept that the experience of the self is real. The actual past that was and has happened can be condemned and move away from because it will never repeat itself. The experiences of the past are outlined as conscience of the self-regulating itself into existing.

Interpretations for success:

Live in the moment. To do so you must love what you do, and the people and things around you. The only reality is the one we breath in now. The past is solidified and defined the future is not and will not be until it comes. Why then do we not live for the now? Create movement that will be the past only better, as we are aware of it.

With loving, meaning having passion and a perverse interest in the functions of your job and the experiences of others around you can you construct a Nietzsche'an past experience. Leading is about others connecting to you, not necessarily the company they work for. It will always be you who they see as the person to lean to, not a figure at the top of the corporate ladder that is never present.

26. CARL SCHMITT (1888-1985)

Famous quote:
"Tell me who your enemy is and I will tell you
who you are."

A substantial deal of controversy is associated with Schmitt. Being part of the Nazi party (although he claimed he was very reluctant) and being against American Imperialism (probably because of being interned after WWII), his work nonetheless is quite compelling. Investigating sovereignty of nations and the definition of 'enemy' his work is a testament to modern political practices and policies.

The message:

There is no wickedness or enemies, there is only challenges and opponents.

Schmitt tried to explain to many that just because a person is in conflict with someone else does not mean we should classify them into an enemy. As well, he explained, that we oversimplify naturally and automatically that just because someone is not us, we are in direct conflict with them. We should look at threats;

not outsiders or oversimplification of an automatic classification system, but to look at the situation in front of us.

Interpretations for success:

Too much time will be spent chasing the fox around the forest. You need to see the whole picture when dealing with potential enemies (opponents). They are actually not enemies in the sense that they wish you ill, rather you happen to be in the way of their goal(s) and are meddling in things that could compromise their mission. The simple answer would be, either get out of the way, or figure out what role you play in that whole scenario.

The truth is, that you do not have time or the resources to battle each opponent and challenge that comes your way. You would spent a lifetime just solving other people's issues. The smart approach would be to either completely remove yourself from the situation and let them battle it out with others along their way, or if it is something that could benefit both, tactfully approach and investigate how you could bring the challenge to a fruitful end. This way you make more friends along the way and opponents relent.

27.JOAN OF ARC (1412-1431)

Famous quote:
"Act and God will act."

600 years after her death, Joan of Arc, a Christian martyr still inspires. Her story is ridiculously unbelievable when put into modern perspective. That a young woman, could inspire a deflated and demotivated French court to stand up and continue fighting oppression and English expansion.

The message:

Find out what you are fighting for. Purpose.

Joan had one purpose in her short life, "end oppression in France". What it must have been for her to stand up to the power of England, only divine intervention, as many believed, could push her beyond the limits that the world set on her. Finally, being captured and burned at the stake for her beliefs it is a testament of what it is to live for and die for what you believe in. With the act of killing her, the English only then solidified the

French into moving the 100 year war to a close.

Interpretations for success:

Life would be so easy if we could just "show up" for the ride. Vegetating and in a state of comatose where we slide into oblivion every time a challenge is raised. We say it's not worth the trouble, energy and whatever excuse you need to say. The opposite is also true, to show up and make a difference. The energy it takes to do both actions actually is not all that different from each other.

Attitude towards your purpose in life is a leadership calling of the first degree. Why do or go into a role of leader if you have no end in mind. What is it that you need to do? For who? Is there fight in you to endure, criticism and blame even when there is none to be had. In your eyes, is there a course that you can take that will keep you up at night, so that maybe you will be supporting a Joan of Arc if you necessarily do not want to be her yourself.

28.MARCUS AURELIUS (121-180)

Famous quote:
"Everything we hear is an opinion, not a fact.
Everything we see is a perspective, not truth."

Perhaps one of the most influential books for developing balanced leaders and leadership, 'Meditations', is a masterpiece of advice. Known as part of the Five Good Emperors, Aurelius balanced Rome during his reign. He was able to combat the weaknesses of the human form with a calm and stoic discipline.

The message:

Cut the bullshit ruthlessly.

Never ending pride and interference of others' ego, the bullshit keeps coming day in day out. Aurelius made it possible to focus his mind on the now, the future and past are by products and unknowns, unnecessary for now. Call a thing for what it really is, as it really represents itself without embellishments.

Interpretations for success:

Few and far between do leaders like Marcus Aurelius come. Perhaps, it is because power corrupts, especially in totalitarian rule. Much like a CEO who has complete power over the company, they take total control and lose the vision of what it is to be a great leader. To be a stoic like Aurelius, it is living as a stoic not just talking or writing about it. In Meditations it is seen that he did live like this.

When you are 'appointed' to the leader role, you may be reluctant to take it. If your abilities are capable of performing at this level, but you find yourself lacking motivation, the stoic attitude would be to accept this, as it is your duty to perform with the talents that you possess. There is a voice in your head that keeps negotiating with you telling you things that you can and cannot do, cut it out and do what is right. Honest action can never be replaced by accuracy. If you make a wrong decision but had the honest intent to making it right, that is all you can do. Your failure might make you weak but it is your integrity that keeps you stronger than before. Leave the bullshit of others with them, you take your life forward along with your integrity.

29. NAPOLEON BONAPARTE (1769-1821)

Unsatisfied ambition along with military genius makes a man such as Napoleon. History has analyzed his every well-known move. It is far more important to realize what he really was, simply, driven.

The message:

You have all you need in front of you.

His failure in the invasion of Russia made Napoleon abdicate from his role. It is much more interesting to know, that had the allies not combined their forces against him and the Grand Army, would they have been able to stop him? Ideas springing out of his mind when the odds were certainly stacked against him, he was able to win battle after battle. Resourcefulness is another word for genius.

Interpretations for success:

It is not the leaders who has tenured people with loads of experience at his back that is considered successful, he is just another manager. It is a leader who in the face of changes and lack of information and resources that makes a result out of nowhere who is considered genius.

Learn to live with a little and a lot will be granted. There is a compelling reason within us to fight harder when we know that we are the underdog in a fight. We find solutions where others only see problems. We motivate where others are done.

Your people will learn to see the value that you place on them, they will follow you like Napoleons men followed him. It is inevitable, for someone who takes the time to learn their people intimately for the role ahead, the battles that await. You need little to succeed.

30.OMAR BRADLEY (1893-1981)

At the height of the invasion Bradley commanded roughly 1.3 million men or 43 divisions in the Normandy landings, or making him the first U.S. commander to command that many men in history. There is little General Bradley did not do in regards to the military operations of the United States, which puts him in the pilot seat of being one of the most competent military leaders of our modern time.

The message:

Prevent mistakes before they happen.

Closely connected with General Patton, both served in WWII, they worked together to bring the Axis and the war to a close. As with any military operation, mistakes are costly and following Napoleon's advice- "generals do not

form strategy but they mold human nature"
they were concerned with winning the war as
soon as possible.

Interpretations for success:

Think twice act once. Leadership is a
controversial discipline, where success over-
inflates a leaders' ability (they could have just
been lucky), and failure buries bodies. It is
essential that when leading a group of people,
through change, that you work out the
wrinkles in your head. Like Bradley, how
many options are there in 1.3 million soldiers
to make a mistake, 1.3 million.

Think like children do. Organization and
adaptation of your environment. Children
make mistakes because they have a hard time
controlling themselves. As adults we possess
more levels of control and can use adaptation
and organization to construct a rational view
of what is to come.

Thinking develops quantitatively the picture
of what will happen. How much will happen,
and where it should happen. Accommodating
the whole environment, you can begin to avoid

mistakes as much as possible or as much as General Bradley.

31.PYRRHUS OF EPIRUS (318-272) BCE

Famous quote:
"Another such victory and we are undone."

The term Pyrrhic Victory comes from The king of Epirus. The battles that were fought with early Rome over the territory of Asculum made King Pyrrhus understand that he bit off more than he could chew.

The message:

Know the cost of winning.

The battles that were waged between the Epirot's and Romans were unmatched. At least in terms of numbers. The Romans had a never ending army, the Epirot's had limited numbers, only a matter of time when the numbers of the Epirot's would diminish. Hence the term Pyrrhic victory. Not knowing when to quit and settle, King Pyrrhus's battles cost him a humiliating death by a falling tile from the roof tops.

Interpretations for success:

Leadership is also about knowing when to stop going. Stop fighting senseless battles. Knowing how much the enemy has that you don't. Much like the mad ambition of Kings, leaders must know what it is that winning will cost them. Hurt relationships, bad reputations or irreparable stress.

If the cost of winning means giving up a part of your soul, then avoid it. Let the other person do that type of winning. Roman's knew that eventually the hold of the Epirot's would fold. They also learned that their army and tactics were outdated from the defeats handed to them. Winning it would seem is not as important as learning from defeat.

In leading, you can judge at a point where winning will take you. If it seems a too high a price to pay, then stop.

32. SCIPIO AFRICANUS (236-183) BCE

Tagged with 'end the invasion and occupation' of Roman territories by Hannibal; Publius Cornelius Scipio Africanus defeated Hannibal at the battle of Zama. Credited by historians as one of the greatest military minds of all time.

The message:

Expect the unexpected.

His purpose was service to Rome and fulfill a military life. His father before him was a general in the Roman army and it was his attitude towards Rome that made him determined to defend it from its enemies.

Interpretations for success:

It might be silly to think that you will know everything, even childish. Unexpected events such as the capabilities of other leaders that undermine your progress is actually expected not unexpected. It is expected that you will fail, not unexpected. The reciprocal nature of decisions is that you should know to live in the unexpected and move towards it.

The caution that you might hear in not venturing forth is a crutch for your leadership. It was never intended to have a leader develop by sitting and reading but by doing the things that happen. Situations are never the same, and unexpected events need to happen. Expect the unexpected to happen to you on a daily basis.

33.SPARTACUS (111-71) BCE

Famous quote:
"A man must accept his fate or be destroyed by it."

Oppression is rarely left alone when it comes to people receiving it. Rome's grip on the conquered lands gave them plenty of cannon fodder for the colosseum and the games that awaited the participants. Fighting to the death, blood was the currency of happiness. Spartacus, one such participant enjoyed the glory of fighting as a gladiator, but more did he enjoy breaking the chains of Rome and fighting against it.

The message:

Live with the cards you are dealt in life, but keep drawing out better hands.

Spartacus' story not only inspires but teaches us that we are not destined to chance that surrounds us. It is in our power to control the outcomes however hard they may seem to us. Spartacus and his army fought as free men against what they saw as unjust, when nobody else stood up they realized that dying free was better than living a slave.

Interpretations for success:

You will never be in an ideal position in life. Something will always conspire against you. Most often yourself and your own weaknesses and arrogance. Leading means that you deal with what you are given. Most often others' problems that you inherit. You work with barbarians and learn to deal with them as well. Bosses pass you up for incompetent 'politicians' in your offices... etc.

You realize that sometimes you cannot win. Much like a Spartacus probably thought at one time. There does come a time when you will be fed up with your own excuses that you will take action. It is much better to understand that whatever it is that you do have going on now that 'sucks', there was someone in history before you that had it much worse and turned their situation around; and probably whining less than you are now. Learn to live with the cards that you are dealt, winning is drawing out the cards that remain.

34. WOODROW WILSON
(1856-1924)

Famous quote:
"I don't only use all the brains that I have, but all that I can borrow."

Starting as an academic and later on as the president of the United States, Wilson had many choices of what to do with his life. Only his passion for politics made it clear to him that running a democratic country would suit him. He served from 1913 to 1921 of which 4 years were spent diffusing the rampage of WWI.

The message:

You are not the smartest guy in the room.

In today's standards, smart means you know how to deal with a given situation. Book smarts really don't count if you can't use them. Wilson had both, a PhD and a Presidency to use his book smarts properly. You don't want to have degrees that you can't use.

Interpretations for success:

We live in a very confused world. Especially at the personal psychological level. We think ourselves liberated and enlightened and all knowing, by the power of technology we believe we know the solution to all problems. Almost pithy in the amount of arrogance we can conjure up for ourselves is overwhelming if we were to write it down.

We in fact are very ignorant, especially the younger the generations get. The actual intelligence might be increasing with generations that are growing up, however, their intellect is actually becoming more stupid. We rely too much on intangible segments for our answers. Internet, TV, schools, universities are all sources that are not concrete. We must avoid being static. Think for yourselves and discuss what it is that we are doing. Static information and undisciplined information leaves a leader alone.

35. ALEXANDER THE GREAT (356-323) BCE

Famous quote:
"I am not afraid of an army of lions led by a sheep; I am afraid of an army of sheep lead by a lion."

Perhaps we will never see or hear such a story in history as Alexander's. Son of a king, taught by a master, advised by ambition- a man who conquered the world. He was undefeated in his military conquests, his empire spanned to cover most of the known world.

The message:

Will your success be the end of you?

His unbelievable abilities and military success's made Alexander the king of the world. He knew it, it also gave him a longing for more. That "what is there else to conquer", feeling. His search for answers ended up having him being resented by his troops, never stopping, never resting, always fighting. It inevitably constructed his downfall.

Interpretations for success:

What is a leader if they cannot enjoy the present of success with everyone? Most of us have this problem more than we think. The feeling of inadequacy in today's consumerist and competitively globalized culture make us feel that we are not complete. Life is complicated and uncategorized, so knowing that we still made something work, but feel empty is a hard pill to swallow.

Leaders for the sake of the teams, need to ensure that successes are celebrated and work with. It is not enough to keep conquering. Defeating foes is one thing, but not to look at what meaning these wins have is dangerous. The hot streak ends, and it usually ends badly.

Much like Alexander and Napoleon, unsatisfied ambitions lead to disaster; others do not share their taste for victory and constant fulfillment. Ensure your leadership and way of people management doesn't neglect the success that you have achieved. Sometimes stopping is moving ahead.

36.GEORGE S. PATTON (1885-1945)

Famous quote:
"If everyone is thinking alike, then somebody isn't thinking."

What Erwin Rommel was for the allies, Patton was for the Nazis. Both Generals when they were in action demanded respect and fear from the opposing sides. His often controversial public remarks were tolerated by the fact that his military genius won battles. Never has the U.S. produced another such commander as Patton.

The message:

Avoid thinking like the masses.

To win battles where lives are at stake, the leader needs to know what the masses are thinking; do the opposite. If Patton decided to be like every other general and be conventional in battle he would have been unsuccessful in a war that was unprecedented in history. Winning would have been difficult and costly.

Interpretations for success:

It is very easy to ride the bus with everyone. Thinking and behaving like the group is comfortable and safe. In business environments, individuals and leaders who stand out are punished and criticized. However, the examples in history prove that these unique personalities and particular ways of thinking actually helped the companies they worked for.

Learn to play by the rules, ethics and values of your company, but lead your own way. Make decisions based on the environment, do not hesitate and follow your gut. Business is like warfare, except instead of blood it is currency that is lost or gained.

37. DWIGHT D. EISENHOWER (1890-1969)

Famous quote:
"'Worry' is a word that I don't allow myself to use."

A strong resolution to defeat what is considered wrong is summing President Eisenhower. Multiple achievement in military and political life, his resume is filled with examples of leadership challenges that might have broken ordinary leaders.

The message:

Tenacity is as powerful as any weapon.

Threatening to use a nuclear weapon to end the war in Korean and deter any communist intervention near the U.S., showed to the world that the U.S. government will not be bullied by ideologies or movements. However, it was not his ideas of tactics that made his presence known but his ability to stick with it until the end of the problem.

Interpretations for success:

People often see, quite quickly, if you as a leader are joking around or are serious. You might think that you have an agenda to get something done, but your body language and unconscious actions speak differently to others. That is, be quite sure that what you are about to do you will put a whole heart in doing. Do not flip-flop with feelings about what it is that you are doing, just get it done.

Leadership is not glamourous as most think. It actually sucks most of the time to be a leader, but true leaders do not go into the role for glory, they do it for progress. Resolution is a non-tangible quality that does not have a price, yet expected in every leader. You cannot train resolution or to be tenacious in a task. You need to want it more than anyone else around you. Your ego should be driving this quality for the sake of others not for the sake of yourself.

38.WILLIAM SHAKESPEARE (1564-1616)

A literary mastermind living in Elizabethan England, forged a style of writing that changed the English language. More than his intellectual capacity, his courage to endeavor and experiment with plays and stories as well as words made his work what it is.

The message:

"Fortuna iuvat" (Fortune helps those daring)

Creation is reserved for the Gods and people who are willing to dare. Shakespeare dared to find out all the faculties in his power to create literature that would influence the minds of millions for centuries to come. His plays are still studied to day, and used in almost every known language. If immortality was his wish, he certainly achieved it through his work.

Interpretations for success:

Relatively speaking, death is quick and life is very short. We only have but a chance to do something while on this planet. It is very pleasant to be comfortable, but it is in feeling alive that is worthwhile. A complete project, a small start-up, a new family, teaching and helping others is but a small part in where feeling alive, like Shakespeare, can exist.

If anything would define leadership, it would be that they dare to do what others will not. You need not, carelessly throw yourself off cliffs to define your purpose. You will find your purpose within your teams and the individuals in them. You will find a purpose in the challenges your company is facing and relish their completion and success. You must try and do, with enough energy and zeal to entice 'Lady fortune' to assist you.

39.MIYAMOTO MUSHASHI (1584-1645)

Famous quote:
"All things entail rising and falling timing. You must be able to discern this."

A samurai master swordsman, Miyamoto won his first match at 13 years of age. He never lost a battle, totally 60 some battles. It was not his fighting skills that made him legendary in Japan, but his mental awareness and preparation.

The message:

Know thyself.

It wasn't the knowledge of the other fighter that made Musashi so successful, but it was knowing what he possessed and what he didn't. In his book, "the book of five rings", its message is that you must focus on your own work and abilities more than others.

Interpretations for success:

Leaders who do not assess themselves through one form of performance evaluation and psychological descriptions, are bound to be assessed by others. Which is usually only half true. Discerning what you need and what you have mastered, it is a skill that you will take with your throughout your life.

Masters of the sword, or masters of people, it is the same process. Learning to time your evaluation properly is much like executing a cut in a battle. Practice ensures you do this flawlessly. So, you must practice self-evaluation. Pick a time and do it weekly. The good the bad and the ugly, and what are you prepared to do about it.

40.FRIEDRICH VON HAYEK (1899-1992)

Famous quote:
"The curious task of economics is to demonstrate to men, how little they really know about what they imagine they can design."

His experiences from early on led him to be a major socio-economic philosopher whose work contributed to the understanding of economic sciences. Von Hayek, lived and worked for economic definition and understanding which led him to share the 1974 Nobel Memorial Prize in Economic Sciences.

The message:

Use less than you need.

Economics is about efficiency, sell high-buy low. Understanding that there exist multiple fluctuations in society that influence economic woes, Hayek sought to understand and define these problems. The work he did on social-economic interpretation of why individuals plan out their economic situation based on fluctuation of prices helped determine government economic policies.

Interpretations for success:

Forgiveness doesn't have a value on it, so don't plan on using it in a business environment. Proper planning and frugal and thrifty resourcefulness as a leader can mean your prosperity with your teams. People don't like leaders who spend more than they need, this includes time as well.

Just as with money, time is something that is precious to most people. Don't waste it. Use it as necessary and ensure that your team does so as well. Economics is a discipline that uses monetary value along with time, which consumes capital through inflation and other variables.

As a leader learn to be fast but precise in decision making. If it will take longer, then have a good reason to extend the request. Learn to work with less and you will be the golden goose for your company and teams.

41.NELSON MANDELA (1918-2013)

Famous quote:
"After climbing a great hill, one only finds that there are many more hills to climb."

Many recall him as an activist, we should rather refer to him as the leader of a nation. A Nobel peace prize, a Lenin peace prize, the U.S. presidential Medal of Freedom and 250 other awards, President Mandela seen it all in his life.

The message:

Come to terms, that there will always be one more battle to come.

The message here seems strange for a person who spent 27 years in prison, later to be released and glorified as a protagonist against apartheid. It is then, strange that for standing up for something you believe in would be so hard. Mandela battled for three decades to gather the country and build his message to the world; equality for all regardless of skin color.

Interpretations for success:

Leading is not linear, never was. There are ups and downs and zig zags of leading that will throw you off your course and even collapse the foundations you built. Nelson Mandela's story is a popular one, but there are numerous others ones that we have not heard of, just as bizarre and inspiring.

If you lead, then you should already have a vision of who you, and your team and your mission is (see previous topics). It is then equally important to know that you will be always facing battles in the life of leading. This is why many quit, because it sucks to keep taking the punches day in day out. The truth to the moral is that many others regardless of their situation, kept on moving and giving their best to survive and stride. The most obvious of these stories is, president Mandela's.

42.YU THE GREAT (c. 2200 - 2101 BCE)

Xia Dynasty

Flooding being a major problem in ancient China, where crops and homes and farms could not last very long, there seemed little hope for progress. Yu, the son of Gun, had the task of keeping China whole from flooding. His success still resonates in the progress of Chinese culture we see today.

The message:

Find a problem to commit your life to.

So significant was the success of Yu's flood control over China, that people's stories were legendary about him. That not resting until the job was done, not seeing his family for ten years because people were in need of him, that fighting dragons to accomplish his task is what modern leadership definitions are missing. This is what the people of China thought of their future emperor.

Interpretations for success:

To realistically be able to endure the tedious and annoying as well as idiotic problems leadership sometimes faces, you really gotta love what you do. There is only so much perseverance you can take before breaking. You must know what it is and then commit to it 100%.

Whether your endeavor is small or monumental, it requires the same heart going in. The effort that you must come up with is the same, just that the epic tasks require more time. The love that you need to find is the same going forward, this is why many leaders fail because they do not have a set objective in life that they see worth their while. When you find it, life as a leader is easy.

Spend some time, preferable two to four weeks assessing the life problem that you should commit yourself to. It should be real and relevant. It might take longer to discover, that's ok as long as you are searching for this one problem that you want to commit to. Once you find it, be like Yu, and work towards finding a solution.

43.AL-GHAZZALI (1058-1111)

Famous quote:
"Declare your jihad on thirteen enemies you
cannot see- Egoism, Arrogance, Conceit,
Selfishness, Greed, Lust, Intolerance, Anger,
Lying, Cheating, Gossiping and Slandering. If
you can master and destroy them, then you will
be ready to fight the enemy you can see."

His life was dedicated to discovering the truth in things. In knowledge he wanted to find out the purpose and meaning of the attributions of wisdom. He discovered that reason alone was not enough to explain the meanings in theology, that they must be experienced and felt.

The message:

Separate the true from the false.

Discussions that involve yourself and your learning will blind you with false information sooner or later. Reason alone cannot filter information that will hurt you. Knowledge alone is not enough to get the truth of the matter. Many prophets of the ancient world as well as managers here now in modern times, separate themselves from the 'facts' and intuit the truth that is eluding them with zeal of concentration and belief.

Interpretations for success:

You must endure the nonsense that metastases around you, the longer you endure fools the more you believe what they are saying is true. Also the more you work with a company who has bad and outdated habits, the more you believe that they know what they are doing. Ruin is the aftermath of these behaviors.

You need to listen and experience your own knowledge. Stay quiet and learn to listen to what it is that 'you' are saying. There needs to exist a filter for external bullshit, rather the reading and listening of others needs to be selective and scrutinized. Leaders especially are prone to being influence by outside sources holding little credibility. Charmers and charlatans will enter your leadership circles trying to muddle your present state of awareness. Only to their benefit will you give in to their nonsense and misinformation. They do this to ensure that you stay clear of their own agendas. Remember, that you alone can separate the crap from the gold.

44.DESIDERIUS ERASMUS (1466-1536)

His role in history has been quite avant-garde, in a time when the Catholic church ruled Europe. A humanist, believing that hard facts and evidence are more useful than dogma and superstition he was not favored by many surrounding faculties that employed and listened to him.

The message:

Revive your learning repertoire.

Erasmus was in a sense, never satisfied with the status quo. Even his own work added weight to his way of doing things. He would conceive and work out new methods and processes for the advancement of learning, more so he emphasized the importance of forming a sound character instead of just acquiring knowledge.

Interpretations for success:

You will need to be a lifelong learner in the realms of leadership. It will also be required that you learn and un learn new things. Learn new languages, both verbal and even technological. Your old methods of learning as well will need to be relooked at and re organized.

It would be infantile and childish to think that the world of education ends with your high school or MBA, it is more present than ever if anything when these phases end. The book "What got you here won't get you there", by Marshall Goldsmith explains that same premise only relating to career advancement.

Learning is non-linear, you use all parts of your body and brain to absorb the information that you gather. Recalling old information from youth to make associations, as well as using social structures to solidify truth in that information. Revival of you learning techniques should be merciless and efficient. Find out what works in this given time and use it until you need to revisit it again.

45. JEAN JACQUES ROUSSEAU (1712-1778)

Famous quote:
"People who know little are usually great talkers,
while men who know much say little."

While he was far from an model citizen or a great father to his five children (whom he abandoned), his work on developmental psychology 'Emile' gave new insights into how we operate as humans.

The message:

People adjust to their environment(s).

J.J.Rousseau wrote much on how human beings are naturally good creatures, only that their environments corrupt them in the end. Learning by action, in 'the open air', was the preferred method to teach children to understand their being. Away from corrupt adults and institutions the goal was to teach children from as early as possible to find themselves and be happy.

Interpretations for success:

To be effective in a team environment, usually it is wise to make the surroundings as efficient as possible. Not having supplies or tools to get the job done, you are forcing your team to improvise and possibly do stupid things. You, most of all must know what it is that the environment must have in order for everyone to function in harmony and productivity.

If you have not synthesized the formula for effective work, it could mean that a factor or two in the surroundings is prohibiting this from happening. Irate customers, for example might throw many employees off their game, you should train or select certain individuals who are good at dealing with angry customers in order to spare the employees that are inexperienced.

Your success is dependent on how you manage the environment and its shortcomings with your team. This is one of the most important tasks of leading.

46.JOHN RUSKIN (1819-1900)

Famous quote:
"When a man is wrapped up in himself, he makes
a pretty small package."

Much like many other philosophers and great thinkers, Ruskin's work and life are often misunderstood and misinterpreted by 'normal' people. His views on the common man, would for anyone, more or less seem despicable. It was however, his desire to define the human soul(s) through what he called aesthesis and theoria. That how we experience the world is much more than deduction methods of scientific theories and practices.

The message:

Be not mindlessly busy.

That Ruskin was a thinker is an understatement. Boldly taking a stand in his determination that the only true perfection that exits lies with the dead. That the work of genius holds only the unfinished and imperfect work of the master, which can never be perfect. The work of true genius is always working for something more and better. These words of wisdom are where our society has lost its direction for quite some time, we have given up at trying too hard to be perfect.

Interpretations for success:

Leaders who are mindlessly busy are trying to be and become perfect. It is a caveat to think that this is an effective way to lead. We are not made to be demi gods of this world or think that our actions will perfect the way we operate. If it happens it does, that's all there is to it. What the romantics are saying, is that humans are most effective when they realize that their road to perfection is riddled with imperfect routes.

It is much more important to see the errors that you have done, than to mindlessly move towards a goal that is founded in fault. Think of perfection as the process of seeing errors and correcting them.

47.SAMUEL BUTLER (1835-1902)

Much of the writing that Samuel Butler did was influenced by his childhood experiences with his father and his school masters. It was not uncommon for the time to whip and 'discipline' for the the 'good' of learning. Of this, his work is often looked at as satirical as well as utopian also anti-utopian. Not being a teacher or educator, however, his work consisted the lessons of proper upbringing and educating.

The message:

Have fun.

Seriousness of conduct can have a ripple effect on many unnecessary activities. Butler saw that the avoidance of cruelty and punishment towards people, has more impact than the infliction of emotional and physical pain. It is not in punishment that people can thrive but in realization of mistakes through mentoring and guidance.

Interpretations for success:

Often time, leadership is not a role associated with fun. Much like a cold cup of coffee, which should be served warm, it still tastes alright cold. Leadership is much like that; it can have coldness to it but it is better when its warm.

Having fun is not to say that you are not being productive. Or should it be associated with an amusement ride type of fun. Or fun that you have when at a wedding. It would better be described as enjoyment of the moments of leading. That the blood and guts that you witness on a daily basis, is actually a normal part of the role, ultimately learning to enjoy the chaos that you inhabit. For in the opposite, it is what it is, better to enjoy it than loath in it.

48. EUGENIO MARIA DE HOSTOS (1839-1903)

Famous quote:
"All men are good when free from passion,
interest or error."

A pioneer in Latin-American educational systems, Hostos focused his efforts on improving educational processes. He proposed that teaching moves from intuition to induction, towards deduction and lastly to generalization.

The message:

Go beyond contextual reality.

We as a species could do great things. Specifically, we could do great things together. When we look at the message above we can see that it is possible to go beyond what our reality is now, if only, we are able to conceptualize our current state and move to a level above that. The 'smart phone' is a testament to that idea.

Interpretations for success:

This is not to be confused with vision. When we think beyond the reality we currently occupy we are using our intuition then deducing the possibility then generalizing the goal. It may not be possible, yet. These ideas are often seen in Hollywood movies, only to be seen after a year of two on the market available for purchase.

While we may not see flying cars any time soon, the idea is the same. Leadership must use their current state and move beyond what it is possible. Asking the questions that are weird. Something like, "is it possible to have media-enabled leadership that never physically monitors its followers?". Things that are out of reach but not so far as to give up on them. We put a man on the moon, is it so far-fetched to put a man/woman on Mars?

49.LAO TZU (6TH CENTURY BCE)

Famous quote:
"Mastering others is strength. Mastering yourself is true power."

The father of the movement known as Daoism along with the famous book Tao Te Ching, Lao Tzu was as legendary as much as he is considered mythical. More than two millennia after the introduction of his teachings, his message is still going strong in Chinese as well as western cultures.

The message:

Wu-wei (non action)

The significance of his teachings are read in business, management and most of all in leadership. His simple yet to the point teachings result in a no bullshit type of modus operandi in these three fields. Not only are his teaching useful now, they are foundations for societies behaviors and economic activities, the

French laissez-faire principles were founded on Daoism.

Interpretations for success:

Masters of leadership, knows from experience that the best solutions come from when they happen naturally. Without force or exertion. The non-action or wu-wei as it is referred to is a way of living, much like Stoicism. You are not passive, yet you observe and study while things are happening and taking in the information necessary.

It is not in your interest to force yourself upon your followers. Micro managing their every move. Even *macro* managing them is a mistake. You need to train and move out of the way. Monitor and adjust, without interfering to the point where you are making the decisions. You are the judge, the customers the jury. Results happen when the natural flow of processes and knowledge combine with experience. The inevitability and probability that something will happen is very high.

50.BERTRAND RUSSELL
(1872-1970)

Famous quote:
"The trouble with the world is that the stupid are
cocksure and the intelligent are full of doubt."

Although being adept in mathematics and largely studying the subject, Russell was the quintessential logician of our time. Versed in politics, education and social problematica his devotion to anti-war campaigning were only eclipsed by his commitment to the study of logic.

The message:

2+2= 5 ... Logically.

If people are so sure that they are the smartest beings on the planet, why is it that we cannot come to agreement over certain challenges? Logic therefore is not logical, nor is it powerful enough to defeat emotions and emotional outbursts. Even the smartest among us 'release the beast', defying the logical step to stand back and restrain ourselves. We then are poor mathematicians all together, if 'logic' is a mathematical journey as Russell tried explaining.

Interpretations for success:

Nothing is more arrogant or repulsive as a leader who 'knows it all'. We see them everywhere, on TV, our bosses, our supervisors, the guy handing out burgers etc. The stupidity that surrounds these leaders is infectious like a virus, almost impossible to stop. We stay quiet, regardless if we see these folks making fools out of themselves. Why?

We do not want to be a punching bag for the next couple of months after correcting them. The resentment that might happen is too overwhelming for us. Fools, logically, exist. More now so than ever before. They 'google' answers trying to 'know it all', behaving as pompous pricks that won't go away.

If you are one of these characters, it is simple to switch back to being normal. Getting off the high horse of ambition and ignorance, you can still be saved. A simple test would be to judge yourself in the next conversation that you have, do you speak more about yourself than the person/thing that is in front of you. If yes, stop.

51.JOSE ORTEGA Y GASSET (1883-1955)

Famous quote:
"We distinguish the excellent man from the common man by saying that the former is the one who makes great demands on himself, and the latter who makes no demands on himself."

Jose looked at life as a reality in which we must use our reason to live. In his work, he noted that life was not about a linear path to a destination but rather a path of constant self-realization. The problems in life are there for a reason, to be solved by us; to not do so is to give up.

The message:

To be better, have more problems.

This condescending and distasteful message is truth of life. Human operation is based on the amount of folly we can endure and live with, not on the success. Success therefore is easy and wounding, for the human soul and its operation. Jose Ortega wanted to say that these situations are what make the human, as long as they were willing to participate in life's challenges, if not they are merely a person of insincerity.

Interpretations for success:

You can deduce yourself that modern society is too calm and 'supporting' of failure and hardship. We shun the fact that failure is bad, it is not in fact, negative. Any adult that has had a job can testify that the mistakes that they made or the problems that they encounter actually make them better. The side-effects of stress are inevitable, because they pull us out of a comfort zone or 'homeostasis'.

Your goal is not to stay in a successful part or phase of life. Leadership is not static or on an agenda of being 'comfortable'. You seek out challenges and change, something that will endure for the group. The group on the other hand, will fight you for this. They don't want more problems, they want less. This two-way street is what separates leaders from followers. You see the big picture. In no way are you seeking harmful or physically abusive problems, you seek electric and creative ways of moving the group forward.

52. ALBERT EINSTEIN (1879-1955)

Famous quote:
"Try not to become a man of success, but rather try to become a man of value."

In perhaps the most used cliché in modern 21ˢᵗ century civilization, the name Einstein is used when comparing someone's intelligence. His work on modern physics and research on relativity stands as one of the most significant discoveries of our species.

The message:

Your only competition is yourself.

The struggle leading up to the discovery of the Theory of Relativity was with Einstein and himself. The years of frustration and defeat led up to a moment where he finally saw 'the light' (pun intended).

Interpretations for success:

The term benchmarking is often misused, especially when it comes to leadership. The problems with using it in this sense is that there are multiple varieties of the same circumstances available. It cannot be benchmarked unless it is the same person doing the act. You, therefore can only compare yourself, to yourself.

Your ability to filter out people's opinions, for they are just that 'feelings' and 'thoughts' of what should have happened, is key. To keep developing as a mindful, tactful and strategic thinker you need to focus on your own principles and values. It would be hard to believe that someone such as Napoleon or an Einstein were preoccupied with listening to the advice of others. They acted on their own terms based on their experiences.

53.CARL VON CLAUSEWITZ (1780-1831)

Famous quote:
"A conqueror is always a lover of peace."

Considered as one of the few who wrote pieces of work worthy of military consideration, Clausewitz was a military marvel. While never finishing his masterpiece, Vom Kriege (on War), his ideas inspired both military and business strategies since its publication.

The message:

No plan survives first contact with the enemy.

The initial plan that Clausewitz was referring to was the one that we put together and expect success from. Without any previous experience or data, he was saying that, yes, you can make a plan but it will be shit in the first execution of it. No matter how hard you try to get it right the first time.

Interpretations for success:

Do not try to do things perfectly. Your wasted time in 'mastering' the planning and trying to 'dot' all the 'I's' and crossing all the 'T's' is going to drive you crazy when you see your plan go down the toilet. Starting a business is much like this message. There are too many variables both that are unseen and ones that are seen that you cannot influence and can change in an instant.

Let's say that you are an expert in your field. There still is something that will throw you off, no matter how hard you try to avoid it. Napoleon made it a habit to think on the fly, so did Patton, so did Rommel, so do the Navy Seals. Do things go wrong, absolutely! You see the truth in the enemy and the truth in your planning.

You want to plan out just enough so that you can get your team started. What happens when the action starts is, when you react and go back to the plan and adjust. The meaning of Clausewitz's saying is that you will never be prepared for what is waiting for you. The markets change, people play politics, the customers leave etc. All you can do is observe, act and adjust.

54.NIKOLA TESLA (1856-1943)

Tesla's are born once in a blue moon. His genius was his biggest fault. For all his cognitive power to synthesize new creations and think differently, he was considered an recluse by society. Nevertheless, we will be forever grateful for his contributions to mankind and society.

The message:

Don't lose perspective.

It is quite simple to get lost in your work. Tesla was sure an example of someone who when working, the outside world did not exist. It is then through the process of creating and forming something that we must be very careful not to lose sight of what we wanted in the first place. A painter must have the painting in his mind before it is finished, they cannot change the concept half way through.

Interpretations for success:

Leading is not about the destination, it is the journey. You need to be alert that the journey stays on course towards the desired end. If for all your hard work lose perspective in the end then it will be for nothing, because more than likely you will stumble somewhere.

The purpose of leading others is to keep them on track. Unlike Tesla, you do not lose perspective of the world around you. Or at least don't see everything as a threat. The team that is active under your command is free to wander, but you keep them on the road. When the problems start to surface you keep them moving, because of the angle you hold.

55.THOMAS EDISON (1847-1931)

Famous quote:
"The three great essentials to achieve anything worthwhile are: Hard work, stick-to-itness, and Common sense."

Thomas Edison must have been a masochist. The unrelenting pursuit of progress and refinement, to endure until it was done is what made him the success he was. A leader in his time, a play maker. Only someone who accepted pain and defeat as a part of their humanity could do the things he did.

The message:

Relish the pain, it's the greatest gift you will ever get.

This does not mean cutting your arm off or doing something stupid like that. It means that your temporary defeat is just that, temporary. Get to work on a solution, find a hidden corner, ask questions, learn more, try harder, be better. Be more human.

Interpretations for success:

Pain, whether emotional or physical is an important indicator for our survival. The stress that is inflicted on our being, triggers many different reactions to that outside interference. More important to the leader is the emotional or psychological stress or pain that they experience. This is an ingredient for success if properly absorbed.

For you to understand is this. Avoiding pain is to deter progress however small it may be. The failures and broken promises of your situation(s), are blessings in disguise. They never quite seem that way at first, but they are actually hiding messages in their whole story. If you are open enough to accept defeat and keep moving, these hidden stories will reveal themselves to you and you will be able to pull out a message out of them.

56.BENJAMIN FRANKLIN
(1705-1790)

Famous quote:
"We are all born ignorant, but one must work
hard to remain stupid."

Being coined "The first American" was not done by accident. An expert in numerous fields of study, Benjamin Franklin did it all. From science, politics to international peace keeper his life spanned an interesting model for a leader.

The message:

Be careful of the company you keep.

It must have been intentional to keep trying new things and keep developing himself into the mythical person we read about today. Benjamin Franklin seemed never to be satisfied, yet content with the work he was doing. Discovery therefore, was not a burden but a way of life.

Interpretations for success:

The fact that you are reading this book, or 'a' book means that you are not content with just the status quo of your own being. It is easy to fall into a trap of comfort and feeling good about yourself after xyz accomplishment. There comes a time, though, that you must again move on. This does not happen with most people. They must be pushed by someone into action again.

The one's that need pushing are the ones you should be avoiding. Unless you are the leader doing the pushing. You should concentrate on keeping a high profile of friends that act as a support network when you are not motivated enough to do it yourself. Your significant other, your children or your immediate family do not count. Most of those are hard to change or get rid of, since they are too close to you.

Your focus should be on the connections that are at work, in the gym, social clubs etc. The 'friends' that are around you outside your family life. Gauge their willingness to positively influence their own live's as well as your own. If it doesn't exist, move on.

57. VOLTAIRE (1694-1778)

Famous quote:
"Every man is guilty of all the good he did <u>not</u> do."

The French playwright and satirical commentator made an impact in the literary world in the age of enlightened Europe. His work consisted of substantial analysis of church and state and their separation of it. His distaste for religion was made apparent in his massive volumes of writings.

The message:

You will be tripped up by the 'not so good' people in your life.

The message is more Machiavellian than anything. From the book 'The Prince', you are bound to be overwhelmed by the majority of people who are not good, or virtuous as you and your goals. It is part of life; the way you play these people will depend on your success.

Do you get rid of them, or do you play their game back at them?

Interpretations for success:

The trick is to strive to be good as much as you can. No dogma or incantation from outside sources can influence your person. Much like religion and religious interference could not influence Voltaire, so goes with you. You focus on what it is that is in your control. Your thoughts and actions, your integrity to be exact.

The fact that others will see you putting forth the effort for good 'deeds' they will resent you for it. Either that they didn't think of the idea first, and now you are seen as a golden boy/girl, or that they are just not in tune with your message. They don't see what you see and you are observed as an outcast, a poisoner of the status quo.

Regardless, of what others think, you need to follow Voltaire's advice and seek goodness for you own sake. Leadership is first, integrity of one's soul before it is guidance of other souls.

58.JOHANN WOLFGANAG VON GOETHE (1749-1832)

Famous quote:
"The way you see people is the way you treat them, and the way you treat them is what they become."

Being very successful as a young writer in Europe with his "The sorrows of young Werther" which was actually a story of himself falling in love, his writing prowess was unmatched. His observations of living life were portrayed in many of his works, more as hidden self-help messages to the ones who were keen enough to understand them.

The message:

There is no excuse for being an asshole.

Perhaps a life coach in another life, Von Goethe is really trying to say that the way we treat others is a self-fulfilling prophecy. Treat people badly or combatively they will rebel against you. Treat them with kids gloves, and you won't get anything done. Be too nice all the time, they won't take you seriously and so on.

Interpretations for success:

Psychological interpretation of society is too broad and too specific at points. Experience then is the key. You will figure out the group on your own terms. The footnote here is that you need to interpret properly. If the group or team is secretly aggressive against you, you will need to lay strict guidelines, almost military type of leadership and accountability. If the group is timid and new you take your time to teach and test.

Never should you go out of your emotional bubble and force feed the group your ideas. This is being part of the outsiders of the social bond that the group has. You interfere with that and they will resent and rebel against you. Instead of being the 'asshole' that they expect of their boss/leader/supervisor you play a role of support.

The leader of the group first lends suggestions then lets the group decide. A consensus rather than authority is the name of the game.

59.WOLFGANG AMADEUS MOZART (1756-1791)

Famous quote:
"I pay no attention whatever to anybody's praise or blame. I simply follow my own feelings."

His music being emulated worldwide and being considered a genius ahead of his time, it only raises questions of what would have been if he lived longer. Dying at a young age, it is unfortunate that a composer of his talent and ambition would leave early. For more than two centuries Mozart is the personification of 'freaky genius and talent'.

The message:

If you feel that something is right, do it.

It was not until Mozart broke from the chains his father and the surrounding community that Mozart, wrote his best work. Until he saw that the group was holding him back, he was just another great composer. He wouldn't have been the best if he had stayed where he was.

He made a decision to sever the ties that bound him to mediocrity.

Interpretations for success:

The examples throughout history are endless of father figures and mother figures who want the best for their children. The fact is that they put the hand brakes on the creative and ambitious side of these children and they put on cruise control for the rest of their lives. The Mozart's, Alexander the Greats and others are the few who tore away from their parent's clutches in order to pursue their fullest potential.

You as well, if the company that you keep is keeping a tight leash around you, you must break free or accept mediocrity. There will never be enough drive in you if someone is there to help you get up every time you fall. You will always be average. You will always rely on others when times get tough.

It is then important, if you know that you are in this position to make a plan and move ahead with it. By yourself. Learn what you must and if there is more training required, good. But don't take too long. Once you see that you are comfortable where you are that is a sign that it's time to go on your own.

60.BOB MARLEY (1945-1981)

Famous quote:
"Truth is, everybody is going to hurt you: you just gotta find the ones who are worth suffering for."

Dignity for human people regardless of color would summarize what Robert Nesta Marley was trying to accomplish. Considered as one of the most influential musicians of all time, his music was made to deliver a message more than it was made to entertain.

The message:

Leadership is closer to pain then it is to glory.

The satirical way of looking at leadership is that you are most likely a fool. Others that feel things are getting to hard, will look for others to get the job done, in other words, they will look for 'Leaders'. Pain then is another synonym for leading.

Interpretations for success:

Nobody ever applied for a leadership 'job'. If it is classified as a job, then it is just another way of the company saying 'we need a sacrificial lamb in case things go bad'. Real leaders already know that the decisions they make are for the good of the group, not themselves. The success they get is an after product, and a way of the group saying that they still want this person to be a leader.

Once the painful processes start to happen within the leading, that is when most fold, quit or blame. How much pain can you take to get the job done is subjective and rooted in the reality that you currently live in. The determining factor of this pain, is if you endure and IF you make progress out of the pile of crap that you are going through, the group *will want* you to stick around.

There is something to say for leaders, because they usually can take a great deal of emotional pain that comes with poor performance, bad teams, lost companies and other adversities. Only something greater than themselves can they endure this provocation of life and others. That is why the greatest leaders do make a difference regardless of how much inflicted pain there existed.

61.BRUCE LEE (1940-1973)

Famous quote:
"Mistakes are always forgivable, if one has the
courage to admit them."

Dying at such a young age (32) it is a shame
that fate played a bigger role in Lee's death
than did life. In pursuit of perfection, both
spiritually and physically we remember Bruce
Lee as one of the most influential martial
artists of all time.

The message:

Training should be a lifelong habit.

As part of your leadership development, you
should take part in 'leadership homeostasis
avoidance'. Which means, that the stuff you
read here, and the seminars you take, and the
tutors and the Internet 'guru's' of leading;
should all be read with a sceptic's eye. You
yourself are the only one who can define what
leadership and leading means.

Interpretations for success:

Mastering something like leadership is like saying that you will be able to breath in space. It will not be possible. Benchmarking yourself against others is a good start. You need to have a plan, a model of what good leading means to others. It most likely won't work for you. The copy/paste idea does not work in leadership.

Training then, is the actual act of leading. Doing the hard, ugly and idiotically necessary tasks that nobody else wants to, means that you are on the right path. Become Jack Welch or someone like Napoleon is not the goal, it is a model.

You goal is to work on your weaknesses.

Do you know your weaknesses?

62.JANE GOODALL (1934-)

Famous quote:
"What makes us human, I think, is an ability to
ask questions, a consequence of our sophisticated
spoken language."

A life without purpose is not worth living. Jane spent 55 years and is still active, in the study of the social behavior and family relationships of Primates. Not only that, her contribution to the active conservation of wildlife means that there is still hope for survival of endangered species. Her work is a reflection of the social behaviors seen in humans and society.

The message:

Never stop asking.

Managers are taught to keep asking the question 'Why?' five times to get to the root cause of something. It is the same to the process of leading. Whether you are asking yourself or others, the questions that need to be answered are always hiding deeper.

Persistence then, is the recipe for success in any endeavor.

Interpretations for success:

Post high school educational systems, such as Universities and Colleges base their educational prowess on the premise of asking questions. Good teachers ask questions; good students therefore must be good 'question' answerers.

It is only with over inflated egos and narcissism that leaders decide not question any more. Ego driven leadership is based on the fear of failing or looking bad altogether in front of the group. Stop asking and you will not look like a fool. The potential for progress lies in making mistakes and learning, for these questions need to be asked. Humbleness then is the key to moving forward, not ego.

63.BOB DYLAN (1941-)

Famous quote:
"I have dined with kings. I've been offered
wings. And I've never been too impressed."

Artists such as Dylan really don't try to be revolutionary in their work, they just are. The music that Bob wrote in the early 60's defined the generation he was speaking to. The anti-war and civil rights movements being the motivating aspects for his music.

The message:

Don't be impressed by people's resume's.

It is easy to be misled. It is even easier nowadays, with the internet promising many things to everyone. Money is the motivator to almost everyone nowadays. This is an ingredient for charlatans that can't wait to seize gullible chumps. Knowledge and a self-identity is the best offense against an infinite enemy such as this.

Interpretations for success:

Pretty smiles, and firm handshakes but you in a state of delusion when dealing with the modus operandi of swindlers.

Con artists come in many forms. They have infiltrated the school systems and the corporate world. Less work more pay is their 'motto'. You have to be calm and prudent enough to recognize and avoid these quacks, for in leading your group there is a likely chance that one exists in it.

You as the leader need to act, and if necessary involve professional help from your HR department (if possible) to root out these folks. There is never anything good to come from snakes that have found a way to hide in the grass where you work.

64. HERODOTUS (484-425) BCE

Famous quote:
"The most hateful human misfortune is for a wise man to have no influence."

It takes a great man to neglect his own ego and existence. Little to nothing is known of who Herodotus was, however, his work 'The Histories' is among the first of its kind. To take on the form of investigating instead of story writing was the first attempt to make true what was really going on at the time.

The message:

Work on your charisma.

To have influence over people, especially in positions of power can be very dangerous. There is a pattern in history of individuals who have used charisma and influence for their personal gain and destruction. Leadership of course is part of this recipe of charisma and vice versa.

Interpretations for success:

Charisma should be a part of you, naturally occurring. It should never be center stage. Meaning that if you alone rely on your charisma and influential prowess to get things done you are leaving stones unturned. You need to actually have other skills other than just charisma, which just covers the initial surface performance of leading.

People are not stupid, nor were they when charismatic leaders take the stage for the worse. It is in the group's frenzy, that charismatic leadership which is poisoned, takes advantage of the 'group think' to do their bidding. Charisma should be taken at face value, literally.

Speaking publicly well, is a good start. Knowing what you are talking about is another step in the right direction. Being well groomed and well dressed for the part always helps. Learn from leaders with charisma and integrity and you can't go wrong. In this book we have already looked at many.

65. TACITUS (56-120)

Famous quote:
"Old things are always in repute, present things in disfavor."

For a homogenous Rome, where absolute world authority was dominant, Tacitus has the nerve to speak the truth of what Rome was really like. 'Rich in disaster...horrible even in peace'(Histories, 1.2). This kind of honesty is what makes any great writer or leader... telling the actual truth.

The message:

Change will be arduous.

The Guns and Roses song lyrics, "Nothing lasts forever, even cold November rain..." is more true to life and leading than you would imagine. Change, mind you, is not easy. It's going against your natural behavior and habits. Or comfort zone(s) and homeostasis.

Interpretations for success:

The actual need for leading would not exist if no change ever existed. We would also still be in caves if change did not exist. Change and leading are therefore, the same concept and linked through human behavior. We live change, from infants to children to adults. It's a natural yet a painful experience through life.

Temporarily can we say that we are comfortable, and only the sick and helpless are truly only the ones that can't change. The leadership paradigm is the ingredient for those who do not want to change but must, regardless of their current condition. For their own sake if they know it or not. It is why parenting is difficult for most because of the stages of human life that must be changed and developed.

Change for you needs to be a planned effort. The continuous and complete task of moving ahead with your teams and yourself. Success or failure, is subjective, as the process of change is unknown as it hasn't happened, its future based. To change and expect success is unrealistic, to expect failure is self-defeating and immature.

66.JACKIE ROBINSON (1919-1972)

Famous quote:
"Above anything else, I hate to lose."

Racism, hatred, fury and any other term used in association with destruction goes away when we see masters in action. Jackie Robinson was the first black player in the Major League Baseball circuit at first base for the Brooklyn Dodgers. He wasn't just good at baseball he set new standards, and doing it all with a target called discrimination on his back.

The message:

Winning isn't everything, but neither is losing.

You want to have a healthy dose of reality every day. The news gives us this practically. Feeding us guilt to know our place. To the person who is engaged in their reality, they are grateful they are not in that other person's position/situation. This is a losing mentality, rather be thankful and better yet don't watch the news.

Interpretations for success:

The maxim, 'success breeds success', is the same as winning makes more winning, the same-losing begets more losing. In sports we see this with teams who have records such as 7 wins and 75 losses. Or losing 30 games in a row. I would doubt that talent is part of the equation, since we are talking about professional teams, and the level of physical characteristics is sure to be there.

If you notice that you are particularly on a losing streak. Whether in finances or in life, the only thing to do is to stop what you are doing. If at the end of your month, your balance in the bank is in the negative or at 0, then stop spending so much when you do have money. This isn't rocket science, stop inflicting more damage than necessary. If the teams that you work with are nose picking, slobs, then work on yourself first to know that you are not a nose picking slob.

Like Jackie Robinson, you are in the driver's seat of whether you will win or lose, regardless of your surroundings. For this then, you need to take accountability that you will win more than you will lose.

67.JOHN STUART MILL (1806-1873)

Famous quote:
"One person with a belief is equal to ninety-nine with interests."

Being one of the first if not the first to start speaking of supply and demand as a relationship, Mill shows us that the careful interpretation of economics has long term benefits. Most of his contributions to economics and philosophy were due to the early teachings of his mentor Jeremy Bentham.

The message:
Mentor at least one person.

Many managers do not think of themselves as teachers or mentors. Rather they avoid being so in order to stay at a professional level away from their employees. Self defense from progress is not a wise corporate strategy it is a prayer for an early grave. However, if one person in a corporation makes a difference it could mean the shifting of a complete market picture. Look at examples like Jobs and Buffet, influencers and mentors that launched their companies far from the competition.

Interpretations for success:

To mentor, you need to be ready. Both ready in the sense that you are technically aware of all the aspects of you field and the way to do things properly, but also ready in the sense that you are willing to share ALL of your knowledge. Not holding anything back, no resentment, no hidden agendas, just progress to your apprentice and to the field you work in.

Set aside a time for mentoring, slow and steady at the beginning. Nobody has a schedule for a 'one size fits all' type of teaching program. Based on the people involved, you will need to find out a medium that will work both for your company or your personal schedule and the person you are mentoring. If that's once a week, fine. It all plays out what you are trying to accomplish.

Just like everything else, what is the goal you are trying to achieve with this person. Do you have a set vision? Is it that you want all of your knowledge bestowed upon them, or are you filling them in? True mentorship, is the transfer of the whole being into another.

68.JOHN MAYNARD KEYNES (1883-1946)

Famous quote:
"Successful investing is anticipating the anticipation of others."

It is rare, in history, that individual ideas are adopted and used to model an economic outcome. It is without question that the work of John Maynard Keynes was consummated and prolifically used in the construction of Anglo-American economies.

The message:

Learn the shifting behaviors of the team.

The saying, "You're only as strong as the weakest link" means that you need to know where the weakness lies. The team is based on factors that affect the performance and output of the company. You are the gas pedal that regulates the amount of power the team will output. If you do not pay attention you will not get much done.

Interpretations for success:

In the course of a project/year, the team will change. It will change often if the company is big and growing. The way you can see this is to refer to the 5 stages of growth for businesses. At each plateau there lies a crisis point where the teams shifts for the better or for the worse. It is the leader that needs to monitor this and keep an eye to ensure that the team does not fall apart in crisis points.

The end part for the leader is if the team achieved the objective. It is not the actual objective that is important here. The team takes the glory for that. What the leaders get credit for is the journey to that objective.

69.GALILEO GALILEI (1564-1642)

Famous quote:
"Measure what is measurable, and make measurable what is not so."

Heresy is defined as "belief or opinion that is contrary to orthodox religious context.". Galileo was and is considered the father of science and during his time was condemned as a heretic. It is strange and even comedic that humans in Galileo's time feared the unknown as much as they did and put him under house arrest. By doing this the accusers (the inquisition), forced Galileo to write his best work "Two new sciences".

The message:

Limitation in the mind does not exist.

Leaders in history were often criticized and ridiculed for thinking differently and challenging the status quo. You as well will be in the same picture. Maybe even put at risk to lose your job for working 'outside the box'. As many have done before, the risk is far outweighed by the benefit.

Interpretations for success:

You will be under pressure to conform at every step in your career and life. The pressure coming from society and individuals who themselves are trying to contain their positions. It is not an easy decision to make, when looking to break free from control.

Do not get bogged down in the details of what you are trying to do. The details come later. For limitations to be challenged and lifted, you need to look at the whole picture/process/company. The ideas only come when you grasp the scope of your "Rule books". In Galileo's case the concept that the earth revolved around the sun *pissed* a lot of people off. However, he was willing to accept imprisonment for his ideas and keep working on them later.

70.NOAM CHOMSKY (1928-)

Authoring over a 100 books and numerous other articles and publications, Chomsky is referred to us as one of the most influential intellects of our time. A human rights promoter, and an avid anti-war opponent, his routine is focused on global stability and fairness.

The message:

Be at up-to-date in your field.

It is difficult not to get lost in the present, everyday drudgery of life. Thinking that what we are doing now actually has meaning. Without plans, without thought. Just thinking that things will fall where they may, in other words, wishful thinking. The same is true for our field of expertise. The stock markets are different, the academia and the physical shape of our planet is changing, so it is with your field.

Interpretations for success:

You can never be really perfect or right in your preferred discipline. Thinking otherwise is futile and irresponsible to the students and practitioners of the field. The concept of leading has changed as much has the process of making tennis shoes in the last 100 years. You cannot be teaching or mentoring someone the ways of the past when they are irrelevant.

You, yourself will have to re-educate and re learn many of the things that leading involves. From emotional intelligence to dressing like a leader, and everything in between. To know that you must stay on top of your field and even be a trailblazer once in a while is to be successful.

71.SIGMUND FREUD (1856-1939)

Famous quote:
"Neurosis is the inability to tolerate ambiguity."

If there lived a rock star in the psychology-neurology world, where cocaine and sex were the main themes, Sigmund Freud would be the king. Although bizarre and even weird, his theoretical and practical research formed a path for further exploration into the realm of psychology and humanities.

The message:
What are you doing with the time you have?

In today's schedules we do not reflect enough on our past and present states. Otherwise known as meditation or path to enlightenment. If, we did do this we would have a clearer and less cluttered emotional life that clouds judgement, and impulsive reactions. It is not the quick mind that gets ahead in life, it's the one that uses its time it has to benefit the whole organism.

Interpretations for success:

Time should be looked at as something more than effective scheduling or management. Time is really a commodity; something by which everything else is measured. Things would hold no meaning if they did not have a time limit attached to them. By which things dissolve or amortise over time is where value of things come into play. It is interesting that we place such a high value on things/money and not enough on the thing that actually makes 'those' things important.

Even if it takes fifty years, to actually do something good it is worth it. Those 50 years are more wisely spent than a person taking a month to rush through something that has no meaning and no relevance to anything. The month is wasted, the 50 years is appreciated and long lasting value.

The works of masters, while some opulent in quantity and others scarce, all have 'time meaning'. Their work, was combined with the effort to take as much time as necessary to make something worthwhile. Hence, the expression –"Time is our most valuable asset."

72. CARL JUNG (1875-1961)

Much like his "friend" Sigmund Freud, Jung founded analytical psychology. In this the term, Individuation is mentioned and looked at; where the individual is a unique and particular 'being' psychologically and is different from the collective psychology of all humans. The psyche is formed into the whole being of the individual, by experiences, complexes, libido, ego, consciousness and unconsciousness as well as fantasy and dreams.

The message:

Use your talents sparingly.

In this world of corporate maneuvering, political and personal interests, talent keeps talented individuals from moving ahead. It is because things come naturally to these folks, that they are despised and worked against. Much like the leaders of the past that have had natural talents, they figured out how to hide these and use other ones that weren't so obvious.

Interpretations for success:

It is often a curse to be good at something and not trying very hard at it. Being a natural business leader or manager is very irritating to others who try very hard at being average at most. These same individuals will try to out 'work' you but to no avail. Once this doesn't work they try other menacing methods to make you look bad.

Since, unfortunately, these people exist you must hide what you know comes easy to you. If you are a naturally good looking person, play down the image. Purposely tone down your brilliance when around jealous colleagues. There are volumes of books that explain these behaviours. You just need to be aware that this is a dangerous road if you're not careful.

73.CARL ROGERS (1902-1987)

Famous quote:
"The curious paradox is that when I accept myself just as I am, then I can change."

Considered to be in second place, only to Freud, Carl Rogers was a leading mind in psychotherapy. Out of his work the interesting part is his approach to research on a personal level. Individual analysis of persons in the goal of developing them for the better.

The message:

You will replace your old self with the new.

The inevitable part of the physical self is that we are constantly changing. Growing, shrinking, thinning, thickening, stretching and everything in between. The interesting part, is that we sometimes stop varying in the maturity of our attitudes and behaviors. Stagnating our behavior is the same as inertness and atrophy for our physical selves.

Interpretations for success:

As we have mentioned earlier in this book, re-creation is a matter of progressing through the leadership process. Anyone who ever made a serious impact in their field or their area of focus, didn't stay stagnant in their role. Revitalizing your knowledge as well as moving ahead of the curve is the key to success.

If you have been having a particular losing streak, or you feel like you have, it might mean that you need to take a different perspective. Much like writers block, there is something missing that is negating your creative side. You should look at the foundations first, there might be something that you have not been using for a while that is a key ingredient in moving ahead. Such as understanding break even points, if you are a manager.

It is inevitable, that for either good or the bad, you will replace the current self with a newer (hopefully better) version of you. If all things are progressing as they should and the key elements are in play (health, positivity, prudence, ambition etc.), you should be moving ahead to a superior somebody.

74. LAWRENCE KOHLBERG (1927-1987)

Famous quote:
"Right action tends to be defined in terms of
general individual rights and standards that
have been critically examined and agreed upon
by the whole of society."

Focusing on the development of morality, more so in children, he is considered the 30th most prominent psychologist of the 20th century. Building on previous theorists like Piaget, he built the six stages of moral development. Summarily the stages explain the sequences that individuals build on in their moral adventures throughout life.

The message:

What if society is wrong?

The pressures to conform and follow the crowd are ever so slightly growing stronger. Society wants you to imitate everyone around you and vice versa. It is simpler that way, they make products that are generic for the whole, everyone dresses the same, everyone spends the same, wastes the same, acts the same....you get the idea. The few who are trailblazers are often the richest in mind, spirit and wallet.

Interpretations for success:

For the sake of entertainment, we can amuse ourselves with the idea that the more we are democratic and free the more we are becoming socialist and communist (only with more options than before). It really seems that the western cultures have been so preoccupied with 'buying' things that we have homogenized into a demographic that is easily controlled by prices, oil, stock markets and the whims of a few elite groups.

It is then not in the things that you should be concerning yourself with, rather with the implementation of knowledge and acquisition of new paradigms in your field. If you manage then manage your own specific way, within the rules and boundaries of the company and law. It is so easy to let go and get comfortable, for that is what the idea of utopia is (what our society for us wants to achieve), in reality it is a pipe-dream. Utopia doesn't work, nor will it ever. Humans aren't built to function for utopian societies, we are too individualized and alone in the psychological sense. For utopia to work we all need to agree to something, usually this doesn't work.

75.JOSEPH II (1741-1790)

Famous quote:
"I am a royalist by trade."

Although an emperor, Joseph the II, the holy Roman emperor of Austria ruled with the people in mind. Removing slavery, and the death sentence, he kept the equality of all his subjects in mind while ruling for over two decades. His deeds are still remembered even today.

The message:
The higher your position the simpler you should be.

There is an unwritten rule in leading, that the more powerful you are the more you are looked at and assessed. It is common sense that the more public someone is the more they will be criticized and gauged. It is no wonder that successful leaders, both military and political, were quite simple in personalities (at least on the outside) for the world to admire.

Interpretations for success:

The stress that you will impose on your followers and teams is natural. It is normal that one person controlling and leading a group distributes an unbalanced amount of energy towards the group and the group back at them. This stress is necessary, it is additionally uncomfortable for the group if the person is arrogant, complicated to understand, manipulative and _____(add any number of negative qualities here).

It is consequently, wiser to understand the group you are dealing with and YOU adapt to them, not the other way around. Leaders who understood this were very effective at their roles. If the group wants you to be a flashy clown that will make them successful so be it, it is in fact, what you signed up for.

The most effective prevention to bad leadership is to stay simple. Not 'simple' in the way you conduct your business or leading change, but don't use words or philosophy, even how you behave that just has meaning for you. Flashing your degree's or experience in people's faces is another way to piss people off.

76.SALADIN (1138-1193)

Famous quote:
"I have become so great because I have won men's hearts by gentleness and kindness."

The main opposition against the Crusades in late 12th century was Saladin, a Muslim Kurd. With his leadership capability both in battle and in political negotiating, he stabilized the regions of Egypt, North Africa and Syria. With his death he donated most of his wealth to his subjects. He is considered as one of the greatest Muslim figures in history.

The message:
When assembling a team, make sure its resolute.

Very few things were logical or measurable back in the times before enlightenment. It was mostly guess work, lead by the person who is willing to take the biggest risks and most lives. Even in these times then, it was more important who was with you, and their loyalty towards the cause, then their span of knowledge or intelligence in that task. It was—here is the goal, go get it.

Interpretations for success:

We have already talked about teams and teamwork. The placement of you team is very important. Call it pre-work before the actual battle. You should know exactly who it is that you need in your team: Do you need playmakers? Risk takers? Analysts? Etc.

There have been great books written on the subject of teams in the past two decades, of which many of them tackle this problem. Setting up the team before you start anything is the first challenge. It would seem that working with ambitious, capable individuals would work like a charm right from the start. The opposite is true. Too many conflicting ideas gather in a place where you cannot progress, that is why you need a little bit of everything in a team to make it work.

Here is a sample of distribution of value for a management team:
20% = Playmakers
40% = Cross functional players
20% = Doers
20% = Supporters

77.MARIE CURIE (1867-1934)

Famous quote:
"One never notices what has been done; one can
only see what remains to be done."

A chemist and physicist of Polish ancestry, Marie Curie was the first woman to become a professor at the University of Paris. As well she was the first woman to win a Nobel Peace Prize, not once, but twice. She is part of a family of intellects that together pool five Nobel Prizes.

The message:
Notice what you <u>do not</u> know, more than what you do know.

Many of us can live a life of stability and comfort, we need very little to stay happy; especially when we are fulfilled with the little things in life. This on the other hand does not fully explain a path that a leader would go through. The constantly changing environment, and the person themselves involves the absence of comfort and the imposing forces of change.

Interpretations for success:

You do not have to be a philosopher, or a Greek stoic to appreciate the value of this wisdom. As the leader, knowing what you do not know is not showing off your wise sage-like manner but unpretentiousness to your team. Only through your imagination and perception can you discern what it is you really are missing in your field.

It would be foolish to think that you are in control all the time. Relinquish power over your ego and self-righteousness in order to broaden your horizon of the expertise you need. If you work in the medical field you can only expand your skills by taking in knowledge of someone who might be better than you. A process of constructing what is already constructed. Adding floors to an already tall building.

78.IEYASU TOKUGAWA (1543-1616)

Famous quote:
"After victory, tighten the cords on your helmet."

Historical data might be incorrect, however, the plans that Ieyasu implemented ensured peace in Japan for 250 years until 1868. Compared with Rome's Augustus, his methods and his military mind and patience placed Japan in the proper spot for accelerated prosperity. Known for his boldness, he is considered one of the greatest Japanese leaders that ever lived.

The message:

Whether you win or lose, the danger is not over.

Being drunk with victory even for a small number of times equals a recipe for destruction. It is then a test for any leader who experiences more wins than defeats to control their ego and not let their guard down. The overestimated reach that many leaders experience with success leads to hard long lasting defeats down the road.

Interpretations for success:

Egos are growing bigger every day in every generation. On average, the population that is experiencing great growth is also going to have to face great disappointment, because they will have to face their own setbacks. The passive aggressive attitudes that many of us encounter and use every day are a prerequisite for homogenous life failures.

It is not then, the instant satisfaction and gratification that you should seek in making you happy, rather the continuous improvement of everything in your life. Your life gets in the 'danger zone' when you think you have got all the cards in your hand, regardless of how much you own/have/possess. There are countless stories of genius millionaires who lost everything because they flew too close to the sun.

After winning the danger doesn't end.

79. SOPHOCLES (496-406 BCE)

Famous quote:
"I would prefer to fail with honor than to win by cheating."

The Athenians were a specific and curious lot. Taking competitions in what was known as Lenaia, or a religious play/drama festival. Sophocles won 18 of the 30 he participated in, often times coming in second place if not first. His work later influenced many of the literary and political figures in history.

The message:
You lose more if you cheat and win.

The modern tone of the youth is that winning is everything. This is emphasized more than we think. We need to have the perfect mate, the perfect family, the best car(s), the biggest house etc. The bullshit that modern society wants out of you. You will want to achieve these unnecessary 'things' by any means necessary, usually in the form of credit cards or cheating others into personal gains.

Interpretations for success:

Cheating seems so seductive at the time prior to actually doing it. The few seconds just before you break your integrity it seems really attractive. The moment (or moments) when the cheat happens you lose a sense of your dignity, almost instantly. The emptiness that you feel afterwards is also called guilt.

The difference between you and the people who seem to keep cheating and breaking their word, is that you see the end game of cheating. Leadership is rarely glorious, more so back breaking work that is thankless. Cheating then, is useless. It would seem irrelevant to cheat when you can only get 'real' recognition from the team you serve truthfully.

Leadership is transparent, your actions are seen even when you aren't working. Cheating doesn't work in true leadership, long lasting leaders work without conniving methods.

80. SLAVOJ ZIZEK (1949-)

Famous quote:
"Communism will win."

For a successful society, there must exist people who will compete with the status quo. Zizek competes with the 'right' political affiliations, supporting socialist ideals and opposing capitalism and neoliberalism. If it were not for people like Zizek, society would be ruled by the few who only impose one idea to the masses.

The message:

Sometimes you must play the devil's advocate.

This is not necessarily a leadership trait or advice for effective leading, rather it is a tool to use when things seem to be stagnating. Creativity is rarely linear and predictable, if ever. To be creative and progressive one needs to have a rebel's streak in order to move the needle further.

Interpretations for success:

Furthering yourself in the leadership development process, you will encounter times of stagnation and rust. For the same tasks that happen day in day out become habits that are hard to break and move out of. Bringing new results to the team and company through habitual methodology is rare.

You therefore are required as a leading team member to bring new ideas and challenge the ones that already exist. If everyone is playing in the sand, then you are the one who needs to find out if playing in the grass is better. The relief from the same old methods will be evident.

Be careful, that when you are challenging assumptions and old paradigms that you step on as little toes as possible. It will be painful for most to even think about something changing and moving away from their regular processes. It is therefore critical that you alone act on these in the beginning, only when discovering a plan that has substance can you start sharing your ideas.

81. AMANCIO ORTEGA (1936-)

Famous quote:
"In the street, I only want to be recognized by my family, my friends and people I work with."

Considered as one of the wealthiest people in the world, Ortega started in the fashion business back in 1972. Founding Zara, a fashion brand that provides modern fashion trends at lower prices than the competition, has enabled Ortega to overtake the fashion market.

The message:
Anything worth doing, takes time.

Some believe that 30 even 50 years to build something is too much work. To keep working day in day out on a project or business or yourself for the next 50 years seems such a hassle. Why bother? The stories of Zara, and Microsoft and countless others proves otherwise. To make something worthwhile it takes time.

Interpretations for success:

Many of us tend to be confused with the idea that we must develop ourselves as leaders, right now. That there is a time limit on our development, and if we don't do it that the moments of opportunity will pass us by. The moment(s) of leading are development themselves. The experience is right now and it is what leadership is, not books, seminars or pseudo internet blogging.

Begin with the end in mind. Not that far ahead that you are making up what you look like, but enough that you can see yourself as someone you would follow. What are these foundations that you need? Is it language efficiency? Is it credentials? Is it (insert any attribute here)?

Once you have figured out your map of progress, you only act and monitor. First on a weekly basis you do self-assessment exercises, then on a monthly one. You read relentlessly and take stock on your knowledge, routinely. You take risks, with the opportunities given. You make opportunities, even if they keep failing.

82.RAFFAELO SANZIO DA URBINO(RAPHAEL) (1483-1520)

Famous quote:
"Time is a vindictive bandit to steal the beauty of our former selves."

It was an exciting and highly competitive time during the Italian renaissance. Competing with other legendary painters and sculptors, Raphael made a strong impression on the movement in his short 37 years of life. He produced an unusually large amount of paintings, showing that grace can follow quantity.

The message:

It is possible to be productive in a short time.

Art is a subjective discipline that is impossible to define. It can take a massive amount of time to create a masterpiece and at the same time, it can be the same amount of time, to produce nothing of value as well. Even masters of the discipline, have their trial and error moments in their peak. However, with them is more success than error.

Interpretations for success:

Any worthwhile leader is also a great time manager. More than a time manager they are productivity pushers. They know that the time they have to fiddle with now is soon going to stagnate, or end up costing them creatively to get a solution sooner. The half-life of an idea is 3 minutes. Use it or lose it. There are literally thousands of books out there on time management, for everything, read the ones that you feel are important.

Here are some time suggestions:

- For each project set a deadline for completion.
- For everything that is important set time aside for it daily.
- Learn from your poor time management habits and avoid repeating them.

83.KING SOLOMON (died 931) BCE

Famous quote:
"A fool is wise in his eyes."

More mythical and mysterious than fact, Kind Solomon comes from the old testament as the richest and wisest person that had ever lived. The major religions Christianity, Judaism and Islam share his knowledge and guidance. His three books, 'The book of proverbs', 'Ecclesiastes', and 'Song of songs' are the ancient self-help books that still hold tremendous value today.

The message:
There is always someone smarter and wiser than you.

Cultural evolution has developed in us a sense of arrogance for believing that we are wise. We are not talking about the ego driven sense here, but the actual belief that we can find out the truth to anything by just "googling" it. Internet research is good but limited as it is available to anyone who wants to write something that

THEY think is right but has no data or backup on the subject. It is in this behavior that we get the cultural norms of complacency and senseless pragmatism.

Interpretations for success:

Being humble is hard, especially for the millennial and younger generations where proving yourself as 'cool' is more vital than seeking answers. The narcissistic approach to knowledge is high while the ratio of actual smart people in relation to the population is declining. You would assume that the increase of population would increase the intelligence and practicality of the populace. The 80/20 rule is shrinking in a geopolitical and cultural sense. It is more 90/10 now, where 10% of the population is pulling the weight of the other 90% and not just in money but in intelligence.

The way to be humble is to collect your assumptions on something and throw them out. Start over in the field that you are, listen to what others are saying and watch what they are doing. Is there a big difference from what you 'used' to do? If there is then, you need to realign.

84.MAIMONIDES (1135-1204)

Famous quote:
"A truth does not become greater by repetition."

He worked as a rabbi, however, dedicated his life to teaching. The wisdom imposed on the Jewish faith and Torah, is significant and still used today. He also made a "how to guide" to faith with the 13 principles of faith where he guides practitioners and non-believers alike to living a better life.

The message:

Wisdom doesn't just come from books.

Often times people limit themselves to academia. Professors and academics are lost in the sea of information that is bombarded towards them, leaving it up to them to decipher the message that they need to preach to others.

Interpretations for success:

Fulfilling the complete picture of leadership is the accumulation of knowledge and wisdom from all areas of your life. A good start is reading books, the best is the form of mentorship and direct contact with the person you are trying to be like. This is difficult, however, often times leaving it up to us to figure out the path we need to take.

You need to be a student assessing everyone and learning how you deal with the situations that happen to you. Books can teach this. Experience is the key. Learning how to deal with difficult situations at work and life is to expose yourself to them, on purpose. You will ultimately fail the first few times, in fact, it is recommended that you fail and that you are humiliated in the process. This is the fastest way to learning and becoming better.

85.PAUL (5-67)

Paul's story is special since it involves special change in behaviour. Being a Roman of non-Christian intentions, suddenly becoming Christian is a big deal. The fact that the book of Acts in the New testament significantly relates to Paul and his life, is an important theological piece for orthodox and catholic faiths.

The message:

Even dogma needs facts.

There is a lot of passion when it comes to the conversations of God and Science. Philosophers, and scientists as well as theologians argue on what is right. Both describe reality of human consciousness, in different and strong viewpoints.

Interpretations for success:

Charisma in leadership will get you started. Possessing facts is what will make you a good leader, because it will influence your decisions. The process of moving forward with your goal is the main objective. To do this it is important that the collection of data and facts become a habit. Anything else that is involved other than the detailed analysis of pre-producing actions is likely to fail.

The reason for the data digging is finding out the 'root cause' of a situation so that you can make the highest quality of decision. You might not be an expert in the field when leading your group, however, the person that you are seeking advice from might be- you should be familiar with what they are saying in order to make further decisions.

86.MARTIN LUTHER KING JR.
(1928-1968)

Famous quote:
"We may have all come on different ships, but
were in the same boat now."

Could racial segregation ever really work in the long run? History has proven that it won't. Its premise that people are different based on the gradation of colors of skin, is a ridiculous idea. So too was the stand of American civil rights leader in the 20th century Martin Luther King Jr. "Judge a man by his character not by the color of his skin.".

The message:
Start treating people to a higher standard than they really are.

To really appreciate any effort of a group of people, the leader needs to be altruistic. Leaving their own desires and passions on the side in order to focus on the group. This is why leading remains undefined and tossed around as a term for better performance. Leading is actually living a certain way, not turning it off when you are done your day job.

Interpretations for success:

Organizations love to use the term, "leadership". It is a requirement if the stock holders are going to take any company seriously. The truth of the matter is, that there exists a substantial amount of leadership in medium and large firms that is weak and built on shaky foundations. The appointed leaders either, don't know what it is they are to do with their position and roles, or were put there out of their own free will; the only motivator being a bigger paycheck.

Not all companies are like this, and the higher you go up the chain the more serious and capable (hopefully) the leadership gets. But it is in the ground floor that leading is most effective. With the direct contact of customers, the employees doing the grunt work of the business. This is where the most important parts of leaders and leading need to be. That is why behaving with your teams on another level of gratitude and grace is so important. This not being soft when you need to be disciplined. It is seeing your team as an essential unit of the business. A collection of core talents that need to be used efficiently; your role starts in the division of talent not the use of that talent. Who is best suited for what, and then let them do it.

87.JANE AUSTEN (1775-1817)

Famous quote:
"If things are going untowardly one month, they
are sure to mend the next."

Not being formally trained in writing or any form of education for that matter, Jane Austen managed to be self-taught. This is why her work is even more interesting and famous. The attention to detail and implementation of her own style of writing made her, even today, one of the most read women writers of all time.

The message:
Don't wait on the jackpot to save you.

Too often we're yearning to get a break in life. For most of us this break never comes, unless we work our buts off in order to get something done. We gamble, thinking that we are going to hit it big. We drink to forget. We neglect our family for poultry rewards. Everyone is waiting on something, while the leaders are actually making things happen.

Interpretations for success:

Ask yourself, "What would I do if I had a million dollars right now?", "What if I had 100 million now?". If the answer takes longer than five seconds, then you don't need the money. Also, if the answer is, "I would buy xyz (bullshit things that you really don't need)". Then you also don't need the money.

We think we have it hard now. Usually we are just being dramatic. We experience first world problems when the real problems are really out there in countries where there is corruption, polluted water, and viral diseases spreading uncontrollably. You just need a reality check.

For your personal development, the question should be, "what else do I need to do myself, in order to keep progressing?", not what will others do for me. The jackpot never comes, if it does it brings more problems than solutions.

88. GREGG POPOVICH (1949-)

Famous quote:
"I can't make every decision for you. I don't have
14 timeouts. You guys got to get together and
talk."

Watching the longest tenured U.S. coach in history on TV you will see that "Pop" is a man of few words. What he lacks in 'media talk' he makes up in sound decision making and winning games. Among the elite of NBA coaches, he is one of the few to to have won over 1,000 NBA games during his career.

The message:

Words don't win.

Coaches get tired. Talking about how things will get done, and this form of strategy and that, only adds to the burden. Coaches know, that talking doesn't help. It's the actual doing part that they want to see get executed. CEO's much like coaches, share the same sentiment when it comes to business, talk is cheap.

Interpretations for success:

If anything, you should set expectations. As a coach, or better yet, the leader, you are expected to set the standard and future expectation of your team. Before you do this though, you should be thoroughly familiar with the overall business and its operations. Formally knowing what you should be doing with the team is a must, then privately assessing each contributor to meet the expectations set out is desirable.

Reality will work against you. You will not be able to realistically finish all your set expectations. This can be frustrating to a first time leader or manager, the trick is to be a stoic and accept the situation that has happened. Learn to set expectations but expect the trickiness of the real world. Acting on the expected then will be key to progress not just talking about it or writing or having meetings but actually doing.

89.SIR ALEX FERGUSON (1941-)

Famous quote:
"Sometimes in football you have to hold your hand up and say, yeah, they're better than us."

If tenure doesn't mean anything in life, neither does success. In 26 years with the football club Manchester United, Sir Alex Ferguson managed and coached the club to over 38 trophies. The statistical observation of how many games and even practices it would take to get to this level again is perverse. It is this rare combination of willpower and humbleness that progress was made with one of England's premier football clubs.

The message:
Alternative methods get ignored once you get results.

It would seem that within experience there is a fine line between being a genius and being insane, being a smashing success and being a total failure. There are always rules to problems that we try to tackle, so it is nothing new that sometimes these rules get broken. The end is that some get glorified and others who break the rules and fail get scolded.

Interpretations for success:

In your career you will hit a plateau, more than once. Where the methods and the training that you have acquired over the years means nothing to advancement of your goals. The repeated pattern that you have used before seems not to work now. The teams are falling apart, and the bottom line is wasting away. Clients seem to be annoyed by you and turn to the competition. Everyone is getting ahead you are falling behind.

For you to stop the cursed circle of failure and stagnation, a little creativity is needed in order to get the results. What this is, is subjective to your field. The important part of this is that you have identified that the plateau exists and you are in it. Much like plateau's in exercise, you need to look at quality more than anything when trying to get results. Quality is one thing that will always be looked at when the receipt hits the table. It is the tangible result that in itself is the bottom line. The methods that you use should be within the bounds of realistic modus operandi of your company/family/personal development.

90.AMOS ALONZO STAGG (1892-1965)

Famous quote:
"I pray not for victory, but to do my best."

It is because of individuals like Coach Stagg that innovations and progress was made in youth football, basketball and baseball. What is more important is the positive attitudes in people that Stagg developed because of his approach towards personal growth. More of a life coach than a coach of sports, the Stagg name is well known in sports.

The message:

The report card at the end of your life is measured in <u>effort</u> given.

Imagine an operating room with a doctor who only gives 50% effort in what they are doing. The reality is that this is more common than we think. We see this behaviour in government, in teaching, in business and all fields of our society. Success then, is more effort than it is luck.

Interpretations for success:

The solution to this in your mental conditioning. Rather, not classifying yourself as motivated or unmotivated but working towards a goal. If you classify yourself as motivated, you will easily be swayed to being not motivated when things do not go your way. At the first brick wall you reach you will be deflated, giving up. You expect everything in life to be a linear pattern that you can easily follow. The truth is that this does not exist.

Instead, look at things as milestones or goals. You give yourself 100% in effort on doing the tasks that you are accomplishing now. No matter how menial, you force yourself into performing the tasks and duties at 100%. Every time, all the time. You condition your psyche into locking in a pattern of "best of" attitude. The results will come regardless, probably you will not hit the mark every time, however, you will increase your chances 100%.

91.BILL BELICHICK (1952-)

Famous quote:
"Talent sets the floor, character sets the ceiling."

Having many firsts in being a NFL coach, Coach Belichick is part of the list of legendary coaches of all time. Out of six Superbowl appearances his teams won four. The most impressive stat, however, is his 40 year coaching stint that is still active. It is not then talent that sets Belichick apart from others it is his character to keep going.

The message:

Always reset to step 1.

It takes greater character to admit that you do not know something than to keep going pretending that you do. The changes that happen in business and sports are weekly, not yearly anymore. To not admit that you don't know what is going on is reckless. On the other hand, keeping quiet people would assume that you know where the ship is headed; it might be heading straight for the cliffs.

Interpretations for success:

Step 1 is knowing what you don't know, and where you are now. Sports teams at the beginning of every season need to be at step one. It doesn't work any other way. They take stock of the talents and players and capabilities of the whole. The decide what needs to be done to further themselves down the season that awaits them. Do they need other acquisitions to strengthen their weaknesses or do they sit and play it out the way they are.

If you do not start at step one, every now and again you lose perspective of the game you have. The tools that might have gotten dull in a long battle. The people that you have, might have obsolete skills and outdated talents. Look at these hidden but practical signs in your sphere of influence in order to see if you need to be at step 1 again.

92. BOB KNIGHT (1940-)

Famous quote:
"The key is not the will to win…everybody has that. It is the will to prepare to win that is important."

Often success leads to controversy, as is the case with Knight. The difference is that his success dwarfs his combative attitude. Being in second place to coach Mike Krzyzewski, knight won 902 Division I NCAA games with his teams. He won coach of the year 4 times and brought a gold medal with the 1984 men's Olympic team.

The message:

Out of 100%, spend 80% preparing and practicing.

When things are actually happening, especially in sports, where we see the athlete in action we only see the 20% of what they invested. Take a look at the Olympics, they spend 4 years preparing only to show for it for about two to three days of action. The four years is what matters, the three days are just formalities to justify their work.

Interpretations to success:

The sale, the bottom line and the gold medal, really are part of a smaller picture. It is not these things that make a company/leader successful but the work before. The meddling and analyzing what will be best for presenting to the customer, the work in the warehouse making sure the delivery gets in on time. There are countless examples for us to see that the small piece at the end of the effort is just the cream on top, it is the preparation beforehand that is important.

Try not to think of work as "work". You should have already established a sense of Zen whether you like your job or not. It is now, important that you see how hours of preparation, (often boring, tedious, and distracting hours) affect the results that you seek.

93.PAUL BROWN (1908-1991)

Famous quote:
"You can learn a line from a win and a book
from a defeat."

Another NFL coach that is more legend than human, Coach brown is the only NFL coach to have a team named after him. Bringing in new ideas and modifications to the game of American football, Brown made sure that he never stopped learning.

The message:

Love losing.

As children we are brought up to hate to lose; that winning is the only thing. The good hearted nature of our youth coaches communicate this the wrong way. They want to say, "don't give up", but their message gets across as "second place is the first loser, and you are worthless if you don't win". This later translates into adulthood as fear of trying, because if you don't try you can't lose.

Interpretations for success:

The successful leader, inventor, scientist and entrepreneur loves to lose. They learn something new every time, and losing is not forever nor is it fatal (maybe in the adrenaline fueled- skydiving, cliff jumping, motorcycle driving and similar extreme areas of life). The attitude that winning will bring success in the future is actually wrong. The repetitive nature of winning means that the chances of continuance of success depletes.

If you keep doing the same thing over and over again, the competition learns what you do, the market gets saturated, and the employees get complacent. We will not talk about how to lose or the psychological recovery of loss, there are thousands of books on that. You just need to know that losing is something special that only the best can use to their advantage.

94.KNUTE ROCKNE (1881-1931)

Famous quote:
"There is no need for me continuing unless I'm able to improve."

The significance of Rockne's life was easily determined by looking at his pot-mortem procession. Dying in a plane crash, over 100,000 people attended his funeral procession. His contribution to a sport was more than profession it was a way of life. Playing for Knute was more than just a job it was an honor.

The message:

Life formula= 90% attitude + 9% sweat +1% luck.

The common occurrence with our society is that we have very, very gifted individuals. In all professions, we are amazed at the talents and extraordinary abilities of those who seem to excel without effort. This is no secret, that these particular individuals have something more than others; attitude towards everything they do.

Interpretation for success:

Studying the mind or cognitive psychology, researchers study behaviors. We as a species have more or less, a set foundation of emotions that we use. Throughout life, we depend on these regulators to activate our behaviors. When we do not develop these behaviors effectively throughout life, we end up making stupid mistakes. We depend on wrong emotional signals to accurately determine outcomes, which do not happen.

Attitude in life, is the subjective term for optimism, positivity and hope that things will work out. Even in tough, undefined sections of life, attitude will determine if you can continue or not.

95.BEAR BRYANT (1913-1983)

Famous quote:
"Never quit. It's the easiest cop-out in the world.
Set a goal and don't quit until you attain it.
When you do attain it, just set another goal, and
don't quit until you reach it. Never quit."

At retirement he held the most wins as a head coach in college football history with 323. To add to his numerous list of accomplishments, many of his players went to coach and stay active in football later in life.

The message:

Set goals only if you plan on getting them done.

New year resolutions seem to be the "thing" when January 1st comes around. Everybody is psyched to get things done, they make plans, goals and other promises they don't keep. Don't be like one of these people. Either do something or don't, save yourself the frustration of failed attempts by not attempting at all.

Interpretations for success:

The psychological association that we humans have with written things is greater than we think. When something is written down, we tend to behave more aggressively to accomplishing these things. When we write it down multiple times we act more consistently in completing it. The same goes for the goals that you have set. Write them down. Not on a computer but in hand written format. The connection between your primitive, hand, and your brain makes a stronger association to behaving in a way to complete the goal(s).

Goals serve a purpose, one better is the behaviors without goals. You should be motivated enough to not need goals, just guidelines in your life to move forward to. If the goal does exist, will it be repeated down the road, if yes, then it is not a goal but a lifestyle change. Living without goals but having strong lifestyles is more important to a leader…and less disappointing.

96. DEAN SMITH (1931-2015)

Famous quote:
"If you make every game a life and death proposition, you're going to have problems. For one thing, you'll be dead a lot."

To lead the greatest (to be) basketball player of all time you need to be good at what you do. Coaching basketball for 36 years at the University of North Carolina, and winning 2 NCAA titles, one of which was with NBA basketball legend Michael Jordan. The saying greatness breeds more greatness is true when talking about Dean Smith.

The message:

Don't take things too seriously.

The common saying, 'life is too short' is really true. Living takes time, and when you add trifling and petty problems to it, life loses its fun.

Interpretations for success:

There are several areas and times in life that you should consider seriously. Selecting a spouse or life partner, deciding where to live, figuring out if you want children or not to name a few. The other parts of life, where the game is relevant on mainly other factors out of your control, you should not break your head over it too much. Taking a stance on things that really don't need it is like being competitive in eating cake, it's good that you're first but who cares.

The opposite happens when you relax and let things happen as they should. You are able to work freely from stress letting your creative side work for you. Nothing is blocking your ability to think clearly and you stay focused longer. The moment you feel that things are getting stressed, just stop or pause. Walk away for a bit, get some air, rethink how stupid it is that stress is being introduced again. Realistically you will not be able to 'escape' all the time. In these situations you train yourself to control your breathing and focus on the subject matter, which in the end, is probably just another petty project or argument or person.

97.VINCE LOMBARDI (1913-1970)

Famous quote:
"I firmly believe that any man's finest hour, the greatest fulfillment of all that he holds dear, is that moment when he has worked his heart out in a good cause and lies exhausted on the field of battle – victorious."

Coach Lombardi is more often used for motivational speeches and references in being persistent than he is associated to football. His philosophy of football was closely related to the philosophy of how to live as a good person. The greatest award of the NFL, for which all teams bleed for every year, is the Lombardi Superbowl Trophy. A symbol of sacrifice, team work and success, Vince Lombardi set the standard for what it meant to be a Hall of Famer.

The message:
Guts and glory.

Similar to attitude, the behavior of coaches like Lombardi are what standards get carved out of. Once the world see's this type of action it is hard to go back to the norm, because it is so contagious and appealing.

Interpretations for success:

You will face time(s) in your career and life, where you alone are the only one standing in your corner. There is nobody else, no parents to help you, no rich cousins, no friends, nobody. Everyone has abandoned you in one form or another, and you alone are the only one who can help yourself. When this happens, you can pick two options, a) give up and be crushed by circumstances, proving to everyone that they were right and you truly suck or b) swallow hard, spit the blood out in your mouth, stand up straight and punch every circumstance that comes in your way in the face! If you fall again, the chances that you will not get up are very slim.

It takes very little to be good or to be bad, it usually comes down to the behavior that someone will act out on. Be like everyone else around you, and you will do fine. Be like yourself, act with courage and dignity, take action and you will be like the Lombardi's of the world.

98.JOHN WOODEN (1910-2010)

Famous quote:
"If you're not making mistakes, then you're not doing anything. I'm positive that a doer makes mistakes."

The 'king Midas' of basketball, everything he touched turned to gold. Out of the 12 seasons at UCLA, ten NCAA championships came out, including seven in a row. A feat never to be repeated. While the success in basketball seemed to come naturally, Wooden taught his players to repeat the success in their personal lives. At the top of his personal philosophy of "pyramid of success" lies the message: Competitive greatness- "Perform at your best when your best is required. Your best is required each day."

The message:

Your best is required each day.

Sacrifice is a word that is not heard very often anymore. Where one person lets go of their personal gratification for the good of the group. For the leader this is normal and necessary. The sacrifice that we are talking about here is the best performance you try to give every day, there are no breaks.

Interpretations for success:

Reading the quote from Wooden explains a lot. You will make a tremendous amount of mistakes in your tenure as a leader. Some of them will cost you dearly, emotionally and professionally. The important part of this is if you learn anything from them in the long run.

It is unnecessary to talk about how hard you should work. Even talking about what is 'best' is subjective to each person. The standard that should be looked at is if YOU feel that you did your best. If the feeling is that you could have done more, then you only disappoint yourself and you will know it. Next time do a little more, not much, and see what that does. It will surely feel better than before.

99.SCOTTY BOWMAN (1933-)

Famous quote:
"There is nothing so uncertain as a sure thing."

Coach Bowman holds the record for most wins in NHL history at 1,244 and 9 Stanley cups. One of the most successful coaches of any sport in history, Coach Bowman holds this title. His manner of leading is the culmination of experience and teaching to the players that made it happen under his command.

The message:

Life is entirely unexpected.

Living is a game of numbers. Like Gretzky said, "you will miss 100% of the shot you don't take". The same is with life, the unexpected amounts of situations will all be missed if you think you will fail at everyone. The least you can do is try.

Interpretations for success:

Being new to a role, such as leading, can be intimidating. It is comical in a sense, because many leaders do not choose to lead. They just lead, regardless of what they are doing, its greater than themselves. They conduct themselves apart from the group and the results follow them, ultimately leading to their group-appointed role. You yourself cannot choose to be a leader, you must be chosen. Deliberately or not.

You will never know what the future has in store for you. The attempt to calculate life's probability of succeeding is nothing but a waste of time. Life is about unexpected events, that is why it is worth living, not because we know what is going to happen, but because we don't.

BIBLIOGRAPHY

Quotes supplied by:
www.brainy quote.com (2016)
Historical references:
Wikipedia (2016)
Books:

50 Psychology classics– Who we are, How we think, What we do. Tom Butler- Bowdon.
The Origin of Species. Charles Darwin.
Physics. Aristotle.
The Selfish Gene. Richard Dawkins.
The Interpretation of Dreams. Sigmund Freud.
29 Leadership Secrets. Jack Welch.
Leadership. Peter Drucker.
Encyclopedia of Leadership.
Competitive Strategy. Michael Porter.
Competitive Advantage. Michael Porter.
Strategy Through the Wilds of Strategic Management. Henry Mintzberg.
The Perfect Courtier. Baldassare Castiglione.
First Break All The Rules. Marcus Bukingham & Curt Coffman.
Great By Choice. Jim Collins.
Mastery. Robert Greene.
Leading Quietly. Joseph L. Badaracco Jr.
Leadership-Theory, Application & Skill Development. Robert Lussier & Christopher Achua.

The Effective Executive. Peter Drucker.
The History of Western Philosophy. Bertrand Russel.
The Five Dysfunctions of a Team. Patrick Lencioni.
Fifty Key Thinkers in Psychology. Noel Sheehy.
Leadership- Key Concepts. Antonio Marturano & Johnathan Gosling.

And many others...

ABOUT THE AUTHOR

Nikola Susnjar is a lifelong observer and student of leading and leadership. His education, training and experience have been revolved around interpreting and implementing the act of leading.

Working in various industries, from retail to academia, his knowledge of leadership behaviours is diverse. Large scale companies have their own leadership challenges, in handling turnover to resolving mass employee performance issues. Academia in itself is rigid and self-serving, not allowing new ideas into the mix so easily. It is in these challenges that much of the motivation to start a new has inspired many authors not just one.

To get in contact with the author, email:
nsusnjar5@gmail.com